Copyright © 1973 by Fred William Gross
All Rights Reserved
ISBN 0-8059-1843-4
Library of Congress Catalog Card Number: 73-76214
Printed in the United States of America

To my family

CONTENTS

Page

Preface vii

Chapter

1	Family Background	1
2	Village Life	14
3	Home Life	19
4	Village Education	21
5	My High School Years Away from Home	23
6	A Schoolmate Returns from America	26
7	The Turning Point in My Life	33
8	The Years in Redfield College, Redfield, South Dakota	34
9	A Year in Military Service	37
10	Back to Redfield College	41
11	My Ordination	44
12	Two Years in Carleton College, Northfield, Minnesota	46
13	Marriage and the Trip to Canada	48
14	Two Years in Canada	51
15	Back to the States—Merricourt, North Dakota	55
16	Hebron, North Dakota	57
17	Back to School—University of North Dakota	61
18	Six Years in Argentina and Brazil	64
19	Return to the States—Lodi, California	86
20	The Counseling Years in Lodi	109
21	The Elk Grove Church	115
22	Retirement in 1962 and Moving to Sacramento, California	125
23	Serving Churches in the Retirement Years	127
24	The Traveling Years	136
25	Some Thoughts on Counseling	168
26	Some Thoughts on the Church and the Ministry	174

Conclusion 180
Literature 181

PREFACE

"Pastor, a man with the nature of experiences that you have had, should write a book."

"Reverend Gross, you have put fifty years into the ministry and also have counseled with hundreds of people, of every age, you should write a book."

"Daddy, you have now put fifty years into the ministry of the gospel in Canada, the States, in Argentina and Brazil. You have made many trips to Europe, including the visits of your relatives in Russia; you owe it to children and children's children, as well as thousands of people you know through your preaching and counseling, to put into book-form the rich and varied experiences of your life."

The above statements could be multiplied many times. Why have I not attempted to write the story of my life before this?

I am now seventy-seven years of age. Many people have written autobiographies at a much earlier age. I confess, the thought of writing my autobiography came to me many times before now.

There are a few reasons for this hesitancy. One reason was the time element. I had retired three times, but each time resolved to take a new preaching position.

The main reason for my hesitancy to write, was the feeling of inadequacy. It is easy for me to speak and to hold the attention of the people. But, to write—this I felt I could not do. In speaking, the element of substance and especially the need of rapport is so very important. In writing, however, "rapport" is difficult to establish. Through many years of counseling I developed and used the method of reading the faces of people, and interpreting their feelings. To accomplish this by writing has not yet become my experience. I hope I can project part of me into this book.

To my wife, Emilie, and to my daughter, Grace, I express my sincerest appreciation for their help in bringing the manuscript together for printing.

I hope *The Pastor*, and the information herewith presented, will bring back many rich memories to my many friends and loved ones.

Chapter 1
FAMILY BACKGROUND

The Soviet Union is the largest country in the world. It covers almost one-sixth of all the land in the world. The people of Russia include more than 170 different nationalities, and more than 120 different languages are spoken within the country. Russia is nearly three times as large as the United States. It is larger than South America; its area is 8,436,000 square miles. Most of Russia is a broad plain from 400 to 600 feet above sea level. Much of the Soviet Union is rich in natural resources. The poorer parts of Russia include the Asiatic desert and the arctic regions. The rest of the Soviet Union can produce almost everything needed for modern industry, except natural rubber, rubber, tin, and a few tropical products.

Russia is divided into sixteen Union Republics; the largest two are Kasakh with 1,059,377 square miles and Russian with 8,436,000 square miles.

Of the six well-divided zones of soil and plant life, the "steppe" zone is a very important zone from the standpoint of area, trees, its black soil which includes part of Ukraine, the valley of the Son and Kuban rivers, and some parts of Asiatic Russia. Possibly the most important reason for pointing out this zone is because the life of my forefathers goes back to this area.

German people have for many centuries moved into Russia and made Russia their homeland, living, however, mostly in the larger cities. In this chapter, I want to refer to two large groups that settled in Russia, one during the reign of Catherine II, and the other group during Alexander I. Both of these migrations into Russia completely altered the social and political life of the Soviet Union.

The vast territories of the south and the southeast brought few benefits to Russia; they served more as a protection for the nomads that preyed upon the neighboring people. The only way to solve this territorial problem was to colonize it and, if possible, to colonize with western Europeans. Attempts to find colonists were made through circulars in 1852 and again in 1858, but both efforts proved unsuccessful, because of insufficient privileges.

Colonization was then successfully brought about by the manifesto of Catherine II, issued on July 22, 1763. The manifesto in substance was this: "Since we are acquainted with the extent of our territories and the riches that might give comfort to many people, we extend an invitation to all foreigners to come to Russia to find themselves permanent homes. Where people are without means, they can appeal to our representatives for financial help."

Then follow the privileges offered to colonists which include the following:

1. Religious freedom
2. Tax exemption for ten years
3. Extension of manual labor for the building of homes
4. Interest-free loans for building purposes
5. Self-government for all colonies
6. Tariff-free imports goods
7. Military exemption
8. Upon coming to Russia, the settlers will receive financial support for provisions
9. Tariff-free export of goods manufactured by the colonies
10. Holding of market days free of taxation.

These privileges remained in force not only for the immigrants, but also for their children. This manifesto brought the desired immigrants. Twenty-five thousand left Germany to colonize near the Volga.

The colonization of South Russia under Alexander I on February 20, 1804 took on a different aspect. Because colonization was not so necessary anymore, only competent and financially better able farmers, as well as artisans and professional men, were permitted as settlers. In the manifesto of Catherine II, no restrictions were placed upon the annual number of settlers, while the Ukas (manifesto) of 1804 permitted not more than 200 families a year.

By 1859, there were 209 colonies established with a population of 125,652 in South Russia. From the two types of manifestos as stated above, it is quite evident that a better element of Germans settled in South Russia.

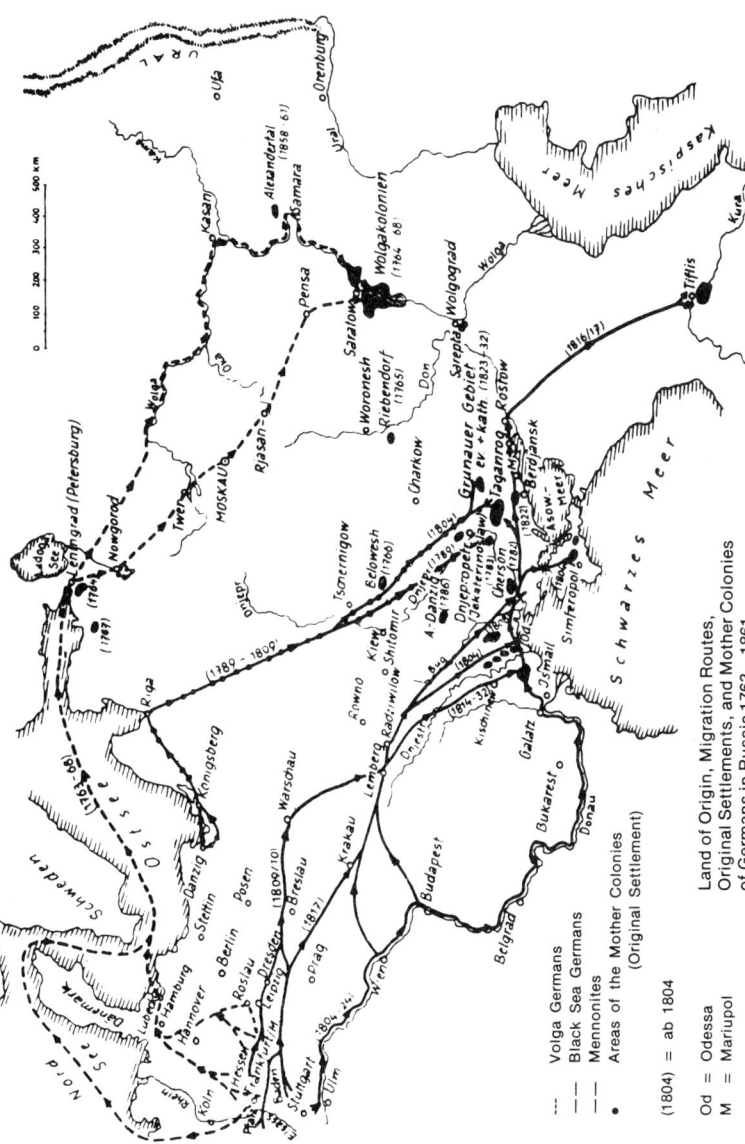

Land of Origin, Migration Routes, Original Settlements, and Mother Colonies of Germans in Russia 1763—1861

Reprinted with the permission of Dr. K. Stumpp and Landsmannschaft der Deutschen aus Russland 7 Stuttgart -O, Diemershaldenstrasse 48 Germany

With these privileges, the Germans were very successful in Russia. Considerable attention in South Russia was aroused by the pietistic movement that had its origin in Germany. This pietism was really an important reason for leaving Germany in the first place. There is an analogy here as between the pilgrim fathers and their leaving England. This pietistic movement in Russia had serious effects upon the Orthodox and the Roman churches, to the extent that the Tsar Nicolas I ordered restrictions of this movement. These restrictions consequently involved the privilege of religious freedom. The result was that many of the German-Russians began to nourish yearnings for another land, a land where more freedom might be granted. America was the land that so many talked about, a land where there was true religious freedom. America and its religious freedom was not wholly unfamiliar to the Russia Germans, for a number of families already had relatives in America.

When later, in 1871, Russia broke her agreement with the Russia German people, which also involved military exemption, the real exodus from Russia began and all eyes were set on North America, as well as Argentina and Brazil.

With reference to my forefathers in Russia, I want to relate with special interest three villages with which I was most familiar: Grossliebental, Glueckstal and Johannestal. Grossliebental was the birthplace of my mother, Maria Riegel; Glueckstal was the birthplace of my father, Friedrich Wilhelm. Johannestal was the village where we lived for many years, my father being a school principal. I left Russia in June 1914 at the age of eighteen.

The villages in Russia still had their own form of government. The school principal and the village scribe were the most important men in the community. In addition, the villages had ten men who enforced local government, and a magistrate.

These are the three villages above mentioned and their make-up:

Grossliebental, like most other villages had, in my time, a Russian name also. In the case of Grossliebental, it was also called Mariinskoye. Grossliebental was organized in 1804. The nearest large city was Odessa, about twenty miles distant. The first years were hard and sacrificial years, with everything still primitive, few supplies and little money. Resources, however, in the form of land, manpower and hard work, were available. In addition to the rich soil, Grossliebental also had stone-quarries; although a brittle limestone, it filled a good need in the early years. With the help of the government, the colonists soon established and developed a village which was second to none.

When I left Russia, Grossliebental was a different village. Grossliebental, like every other village, had a church and a school in the center of town. In the case of Grossliebental, the church was a building visible from every corner of the village, a two-story structure with a seating capacity of six to seven hundred people, with a beautiful chancel and an organ in the rear of the church. Next to the church was the parsonage, on a large area of land with many fruit trees and a vegetable garden. On the other side of the church was a high school (Zentral-Schule), two stories high, with classrooms and a men's dormitory. Next to the high school was the village chancery office, and next to it the scribe's office and teachers' homes. In front of all of these buildings was a lengthy walk with trees on either side, making this walk a beautiful promenade, liberally used in the cool of the evening by both old an young.

In addition to these most important buildings and institutions, this village had an orphanage, a savings bank, a high school for girls, a cheese factory, a large bakery and, near the river, a public water and steambath building that was heavily used in my time. In close proximity to the village were vineyards, nut trees and further out from the village, rich grainlands. With the two high schools and the public school, the village constructed some of the finest homes for the teachers.

The high school for men in Grossliebental was noted far and wide for its importance in preparing future teachers for the German schools. My father attended this school in his day. My elder brother attended it and I attended it for three years, before leaving for the United States.

Grossliebental was a village of very proud people. The people of Grossliebental prided themselves in the fact that they lived in a more modern village, on the average with a better education, and, with the means they had, could dress better than most other villagers.

The church (Evangelical Lutheran) played an important role in the village and the pastor was a man of authority. The program of the church was strictly adhered to. With the school principal, all details of education and religious practices were carried out from year to year. The pastor invariably had two or more churches in his parish. In the absence of the pastor, the school principal (*Kuester-Lehrer*) read the sermon on Sunday mornings; he also, in the absence of the pastor, taught confirmation school. Confirmation, however, was always carried out by the pastor. For each teen-ager, confirmation was a high point in his life. Not being confirmed reflected upon the person a feeling of disgrace. After confirmation, every youngster felt he was now a person of responsibility, with definite privileges and a standing in the village community.

The next high point in the life of a young person was the event of marriage. There was often strong rivalry among the young people in the village. The young people of one side of the village were jealous of their young people, especially of the girls. If one young man had a girlfriend in the other part of the village, he had to be careful lest some harm come to him. Sometimes it came to fights and hard blows. For this reason, the young man had to call on his girlfriend at night instead of in the afternoon. If the young people had an organization (as was often the case in villages) that was maintained by dues, the young man seeking a girlfriend in the part of the village where she lived, had to pay the dues in order to have freedom in calling on his girlfriend.

In cases of youth problems, such as quarrels among the young, moral or even minor crimes, the pastor was called first. He then, with other men of good standing and authority in the village, stepped in to solve the problems. In other, more critical cases, the district official was called in. In most cases, problems were solved locally.

Other rivalries often developed between the village non-high-school youth in Grossliebental and those attending the high school, invariably because of romances between out-of-town high schoolers attending the high school and a local girl. High school men were often referred to in a non-complimentary term as "bazaar hengste" (market stallions). Romances between local girls and non-local high school men happened rather frequently. My own father, who came from a village far from Grossliebental, married a local girl, Maria Riegel.

Friedrich Wilhelm and Maria Gross, parents of the author.

To control and keep the high school men on the straight and narrow path, strict rules were constantly enforced, both in school and away from school. Even on Sunday, the students were expected to attend church regularly. It was mandatory for all students to first assemble on the school grounds before the church services began, by lining up and counting off: one, two, one, two, in a military fashion, the "twos" stepping back and to the right, thus forming a column of two, and then marching into church to their reserved places. And, even in church, an usher would always keep close watch over them.

Another practice in church that remained unforgettably in my mind was in respect to prospective marriage partners. The young people had to register with the school master (Kuester-Lehrer), indicating the date of their marriage, early enough so that it could be announced from the pulpit at least three Sundays before the marriage date. The pastor or the Kuester-Lehrer would announce from the pulpit after the sermon that so and so, naming the partners, were to be married, adding that if anyone had any information indicating that it would be a "have-to-get-married case," the announcement would *not* state "ehelich, ledich" (legitimate wedlock), but simply state the date of marriage. At the wedding, the bride would then not wear a veil. This was a strong deterrent to promiscuity, for the village people looked down upon such a couple.

Grossliebental, among many notable institutions and places of beauty, also had a large cemetery outside the village, well-kept and decorated with shrubs and flowers. The tombstones all bore inscriptions of the deceased, indicating the name, date of birth and date of death. Invariably, the stone also had a biblical inscription. On Sundays, both old and young would take walks through the cemetery, reading names and inscriptions. To keep the cemetery tidy was not a duty, but a privilege. Not infrequently, strolling through the cemetery offered an opportunity to get acquainted with the opposite sex.

Grossliebental, a village about eighteen miles from Odessa, with a population of about seven thousand, rich, beautiful, and proud, experienced a sad future, as I shall describe in a later chapter.

Glueckstal, (The Lucky Village) where my father, Friedrich Wilhelm, was born, was farther away from Odessa, about seventy miles. It was organized about 1804, the majority of the settlers coming from Wuertemberg, Germany. Only 3 families came at first. They were followed by 67 families, and by the end of 1809, there were 106 families in all, or 618 souls.

With the liberal privileges given them by Alexander I, this colony, too, prospered and grew in number and in reputation. The beginning was hard, but the German people liked hard work and were noted for diligence. At the beginning, their homes were simple, built with reed and mud. By the time I became acquainted with Glueckstal, lived there for a number of years, attended school and with my father took many wagon trips to Teraspol, the village had grown to a population of three to four thousand.

As in all the villages, the churches and schools took the center place in the community, with the pastor and school master the important men of the village. They saw to it that the Word of God (*das Wort*) was not only preached, but also taught in the public school. When a new pastor was assigned to the parish, the people would welcome him by fixing up the dirt road leading into the village, leveling it and then sending a few dozen wagons and riders to meet him and accompany him into the village. At the parsonage, an elaborate feast was awaiting him and his family. Every pastor and every teacher was provided with a roomy home.

Glueckstal, like all other German villages, had a cemetery. In Glueckstal, the cemetery was next to the church, surrounded by a wall. What made Glueckstal progress so fast in housing was the existence of a rich stone-quarry. It was a soft limestone that could be cut to desired size. The villagers would cut the stone into 6 x 6 x 16 sizes and, with this size pieces, some of the finest buildings were put up, buildings that would last for centuries. The roofs of the houses were of two types: flat tile, and reed. The reed roof was about six inches thick and tied down with heavy oiled rope; it was placed in such a way that the finished roof would show only the ends of the reed. It was common to see storks on the reed roofs making nests on the gable to hatch their young.

Glueckstal also had an extensive area of forests a few miles out of the village that had good usable timber, but was also infested with non-poisonous snakes. I remember well how we young people would walk out to the forest to hunt and kill these snakes, using a long stick with a sharp nail at the end, piling up the snakes for people to see the results of our Sunday afternoon sport.

In Glueckstal, I became acquainted with the first cooperative. For a brief period, my father was managing it. Many times, he would have to drive to Odessa and make purchases, taking along the eggs and butter that were taken in by the store in exchange for goods purchased. The people, at first, were reluctant to buy from the cooperatives, because the prices were set. The buyers were used to buying from the Jewish stores where they could bargain with the storekeeper.

Johannestal. This village was established in 1820 with 34 families, in all 130 souls. Since there were no houses, they were living with families in the nearby village of Rohrbach until the sod-houses in Johannestal were built. The village was 100 *Werst* from Odessa (a werst has 3,500 feet). The soil of this area was unsuited for grapes in large scale and trees. The village also had stone-quarries, which were later used to build more durable dwellings.

The three dams and a creek were a boon for the stock in Johannestal; all three dams were plentiful with three kinds of fish. In the summertime, these dams were heavily used by the large herds of stock driven out every morning by the herdsmen.

We lived in Johannestal for fifteen years. By this time, the village population had grown to about 2,000 souls. We moved to Johannestal about 1899. I saw the village grow, and became acquainted with average village life, customs, and village progress. The two rows of houses were far apart and through the center flowed a creek with a number of crossings that often became jammed with the ice-flow in the springtime.

There was no resident pastor here. It was a parish consisting of three churches. My father was the school principal, taught school in German and Russian, read the sermon on Sunday mornings and also played the organ in church; the church was again, as in other places, in the center of the village.

The school, the teachers' homes and the rest of the buildings, such as sheds, barns, hogpens and chicken coops, all in one, were an L-shape. The classrooms and the two living rooms faced the street, and the rest of the buildings reached into the yard. We had a number of acres of which we made good use: first, a large yard, a stone wall and behind the wall the field for garden and small grain.

Behind the wall, we had the hay-stack and a straw-stack. The straw, however, was brought by the villagers who each had to donate to the teacher one load of straw a year. We had about a dozen cows, pigs, chickens, ducks, geese, but no horses. When we needed some, we asked some of the farmers to lend us a team for a day. To store our vegetables, pickles, milk and wine, an outdoor underground cellar was constructed. A cellar of this kind was indispensable. A whole year's provisions were preserved and the monetary value of these saved items was tremendous.

The buildings all had an upper story (*Speicher*) used to store grain for the year. Only strong men were able to carry the hundred-pound sacks in great quantities up the fifteen-step ladder. Hundreds of bushels of grain were stored upstairs. Toward spring, the farmers would clean the grain upstairs with a swinging sieve. The piles of grain in this loft were also used to store fresh grapes and other perishable fruit. Many times, my mother would come down from upstairs, bringing with her some delicacies to surprise us.

A daily chore in the summertime, one we did not enjoy very much as youngsters in the family, was collecting the cow droppings from the pasture. The droppings were placed on the wall to dry and later used for fuel. Additional fuel used in homes was straw that was carried into the kitchen to heat the built-in ovens. The best fuel used in the homes was processed in the spring by spreading the collected manure on a 50 x 50 area, four inches thick, to dry. When dry enough, it was cut into 12 x 12 squares and set upright to dry. The next stage was to set it up with two pieces on the bottom and one piece on the top. Then, it was stacked up in five pieces, and when the manure squares were fully dry, the manure was set into a high stack like bricks. To save the manure stack from breaking down by heavy rains, an outer coat of fresh manure was applied. Thus, the families had good and very inexpensive, necessary fuel for the whole year.

The large yard in front of our home was swept clean every Saturday, a chore carried out weekly by every family in the village.

Johannestal also had an ice-cellar in our yard, for the various needs of the community. This cellar was about 15 x 15, and 15 feet in the ground. This cellar was filled to the top with ice, cut in the winter and stored here, with a thick coat of straw on top to keep it from melting.

Next to the school and the teachers' homes, there was housed the village scribe and his family. He, too, had a big yard, but of special importance was a large barn for the ten bulls of special breed that were alternately mixed with the cows every morning. We youngsters in the neighborhood had an exciting time every night when the cows came home, watching the bulls, who were always last, going to their stalls, because they would invariably get into a locking of horns.

As I think back of Johannestal and the many interesting experiences there, one special event, possibly doubted by many, was when my father and I drove to Landau, about twelve miles away and also, in our terms, a county seat, to which the village teachers were often called to get agricultural information, where for the first time I saw artificial insemination of the cows.

Johannestal also had a cooperative started while I was there. Aside from the many duties my father had, he was requested to be the bookkeeper of the store. The cooperative had a slow start, for the same reasons as elsewhere, because the customers could not bargain as they were accustomed to doing in the Jewish stores. When I left Johannestal, the cooperative was doing a good business. Aside from keeping books, my father had to do the buying for the cooperative. The system of packing eggs and butter into the wagon without springs always intrigued me. To pack thousands of eggs first into the bottom of the wagon and the heavy butter on top seemed incredible to me. Again and again, I watched how the store clerk would place a layer of straw at the bottom of the wagon and then the thousands of eggs on top, and on top of the eggs, he would strew chaff to fill the spaces, and so on, layer after layer, sometimes as many as ten layers. After the last layer and the chaff and again the straw, the clerk would bring balls and balls (ten pounds each) of butter, until the wagon was heaping full. The more eggs and butter my father would bring, the less cash he would need to make the purchases of whatever the store had to sell, including yard goods.

An interesting event took place when I worked in the cooperative for a while. The women making purchases in the store were requested, when bringing butter in exchange for goods, to thoroughly wash the butter and then wrap it in parchment. In the store, after the butter was weighed, we clerks would pitch the ball of butter onto another table a few feet away. If the butter was not totally free of water, it would break apart, to the utter embarrassment of the customer. To amend the embarrassment, the housewife would take her butter into the basement to thoroughly wash it, and then bring it up to be put on the scale again.

A very commendable thing most larger villages would annually do, was to collect grains and store them in a large building to make up for the periodical crop failures. To my memory, of the years in Russia, I do not remember any time when the people in the village were in want. Knowing their Bible, they remembered how Joseph had given Pharaoh the advice to store up grain for the coming lean years.

Chapter 2

VILLAGE LIFE

The German villages, small or large, had very few non-German people living in them. The Jews, however, who were usually storekeepers, were always found where the Germans lived. The German people liked to trade with them and make bargains, which both customer and owner liked to do.

The form of government in the villages was also the same: a mayor, assistant mayor (*Oberschulz* and *Schulze*), a scribe (*Schreiber*), and *Zehner* (coming from the word "ten"). These ten men of the village, with the help of the above-named officers and the school principal, would enforce the laws and settle the many disputes arising in village life.

The church and school were one. There was never a question about not belonging or not going to church. The church and school were the heart of village life. Church services were at eleven o'clock (no Sunday School). The bells would ring, reminding the people it would soon be time to go to church. As a rule, there were three bells; the first bell would ring one hour before eleven o'clock, the second bell (a larger one) would ring at ten-thirty. At eleven o'clock, all three bells (the third still larger) would ring together. As soon as the bells stopped, the services began with the organ playing. My father was the organist in Johannestal. The singing in the church was always done with the congregation seated. The congregation arose only for the reading of Scriptures, for the Creed, and for prayer.

On Sunday afternoons, the young people, after confirmation, would gather for further religious instruction, which lasted just one hour, with the attendance always recorded. This practice lasted from two to three years, depending upon local regulations. After this brief Sunday afternoon religious obligation, the young people still had plenty of time for recreation and social gatherings.

Speaking of bells in the churches, they were used also at other times. When someone died, a bell would ring. In the case of a child, the smallest bell would ring; in the case of a young person, the middle-sized bell would ring, and in the case of an adult, the large bell rang. Thus, people gained certain information about the age of the deceased. In severe storms and blizzards, the bells would also ring throughout the night.

There was one other bell, a hand-bell, which the town crier Büttel would use when special information was to be brought to the attention of the villagers. There were no other local news media to inform the villages. If a village meeting was to take place, either social, political or even church, the town crier would walk through the street, ringing his bell, then stop and announce the message. He then again walked about two blocks, again stopped and announced his message. At times, a special letter, from out of town, religious, or one of interest to all, was handed on from family to family. A "Himmels-Brief" (letter of heaven) was very often circulated and talked about in the village. Such a letter, the nature of which was often startling in content, was at times also of great help to the villagers. These letters were often without a signature, but thought of by the villagers as not to be ignored.

The public school was compulsory in all the villages, but only up to eighth grade. The majority of the children did not go on to higher education, only in rare cases. During my later years, from 1910 on (I left Russia in 1914), more village young people went on to higher schools of learning. In my case, Mother and the children moved to Grossliebental so that we could continue our education while Father remained in the village to carry on his duties. This demanded much sacrifice, but Mother would always say, "Education cannot be taken from you."

An important practice in the village school life, aside from the daily school program, was the mandatory handiwork of all sorts, by schoolchildren and young adults. Once a year, a display of handiwork took place in the school. Because a parish usually consisted of more than one church, two and more villages would bring their items to one place for display and for sale. The money realized was used in the parish.

The young people in the village had many social gatherings. They had opportunity during the nights to attend lectures given by the school superintendent. They organized community choirs. On Sunday afternoons, they had the opportunity to take in dances, or take strolls to the cemetery and read the gravestones. The boys took the greatest interest in baseball. The bats and the balls were all handmade. The older boys took special interest in horses and, therefore, had Sunday afternoon horse-racing. Other young elements used Sunday afternoon and Sunday nights to gather in the beer halls. If the young man wanted to be part of that group, he had to pay an entrance fee; thus, he would be able to drink as much as he wanted without paying.

The villagers were invariably all farmers, growing grain, corn, all sorts of vegetables, sunflowers, grapes (more or less); and processing the cabbage into sour-kraut, grapes into wine, and selling their products in the market. The weekly market was, therefore, an important place. Anything could be sold, bought or traded at this market, even horses and cows. To this day, the marketplaces are very important in Russia and wherever you find Russia Germans in large numbers.

A special event in the village life was the annual butchering day. On the designated day, early in the morning, an out-of-door large-sized kettle was set up and fire put under it. Depending upon the size of the family, a number of pigs and a steer would be prepared weeks ahead of time, to be processed on this day. Friends or neighbors would come to help, for there was so much to do on this day; outside and in the kitchen, personnel was needed to do all the work in one day. After the pig was killed, it was placed into a trough of boiling water and with two ropes under the victim, turned again and again so that the hair would come off freely. The bristles on the back of the animal were saved and later used to make brushes. The next step was to open the carcass and withdraw the intestines, to be processed, and later used as cases for sausage. The meat was cut up into hams and bacon, and the rest was cooked. A special evening meal was prepared to which guests were invited to enjoy themselves with eating and drinking.

Each villager had his own smokehouse in the loft—a walk-in smokehouse for the sausage, the hams and the bacon. Sometimes even geese and ducks were butchered and smoked, to the delight of the eater. With the many vegetables every year, the grain, and the meat, the villagers were never starving.

The villager, either by himself or with hired help, hauled the excess grain into the city and sold it there. This was, up to my time, always done with horse-drawn wagons. It often took a number of days to make these caravan deliveries. To load and unload was hard work. The sacks were large and held about two hundred pounds. The young people in the villages always competed with each other as to who could do the loading of grain sacks in the shortest period of time.

The threshing season was also very interesting. The farmer had his acreage at scattered places, thus had to do much driving to seed his crop, harvest and finally haul it to his home place for threshing. To haul the harvested grain into the village, long grain-racks were used, with the neighbors helping, because hauling was so time-consuming. In earlier years, at the time when I left, the grain was hauled into the yard and from there spread on a prepared hard soil to be tramped by horses hitched to a corrugated heavy stone, thus threshing it until the straw could be easily separated from the chaff. The following morning, as early as three o'clock, the cleaning of the grain took place, with a wind-blown machine, and the grain poured into sacks.

Later, threshing machines were used; first horse-drawn, then self-propelled large rigs. When these big threshing machines came into use, many people were needed at threshing time. The straw was piled (horse-drawn) into straw-stacks as high as fifty feet. The chaff was piled up in smaller stacks and finally the clean grain received into large sacks. Hauling the grain from the distant fields and pitching bundles into the machine required many men. The neighbors would, therefore, always help.

The threshing season was a happy season. Crop failures were few. To maintain the normal happy life and to fall back on the daily needs of the family in time of crop failures, the villagers provided a large granary to store thousands of bushels of wheat. Each farmer had to donate a certain number of bushels each year to fill the storehouse for the needy day.

The village life was a happy life. Young and old enjoyed themselves. The old people were respected and looked up to for counsel and advice. The young people had good times and their social life was ample to keep them satisfied. The old people did much visiting with each other and related endlessly their experiences and recalled the important events in the lives of their forefathers. Invariably, some families had friends or even relatives living in the United States, and when letters came from friends in America, it was special news to hear of the wonderful free land and the country where everything was possible. So, slowly, the hearts of many began to yearn for America, especially since the time was gradually nearing when these good days in Russia would come to an end. And, they did come to an end, as we shall shortly see in succeeding chapters.

Chapter 3
HOME LIFE

My father's name was Friedrich Wilhelm. My mother's name was Maria, nee Riegel. There were six children: Viktor Immanuel, Friedrich Wilhelm, Ida, Edmund, Paul and Helen.

My father, a teacher, was a rather quiet man, tall (a little over six feet), not heavy, with dark hair; a well-educated man and liked in the community. He was not a disciplinarian. As children, we were not as close to him as we might have expected. I feel it was not his nature to be very affectionate. He did spend some time with us, but it was rather difficult to really bring us into his confidence.

My mother was different. She was short and rather fleshy. She had a good complexion and blond hair. Her whole personality was outgoing. She was a great singer, and in company very conversational. Her family was well-to-do and had a good standing in the village of Grossliebental. Father met her while he went to school in her village. Mother was always the intermediary in the home, and the children felt free to come to her with their problems. We all loved her deeply. Her love and counsel, her whole personality and resourcefulness, we all cherished endlessly.

In our home, there was always the daily devotion to Bible-reading and prayer. When my eldest brother, Viktor, left for higher education in Grossliebental, Mother always remembered him in her prayers. It impressed me so much that when I left for the same village for further education, I felt Mother would be praying for me too. Although we were of the Evangelical Lutheran faith, my parents often attended the local Baptist prayer meetings.

At home. we all had our daily chores to do. Our home had many rooms and the yard was large. With my elder brother away in school and the rest of the siblings still much younger, I had to be mother's helper in the house. She taught me how to scrub the floors (wooden), help with the dishes, and, what I will never forget, knead dough for the baking, sometimes as many as eight loaves of bread. There was much work outside, taking care of the cows, the chickens, the pigs, the ducks, the geese, and cleaning the yard. Some of my brothers were of great help outside. Then, in a large household, there were the chores of making butter, cheese, washing, carrying in fuel for heating, gathering the eggs, et cetera. With me working inside the house so much, I became very close to my mother. She would confide in me very much since I was the eldest in the home with Viktor in school.

Mother was a lover of flowers. Our house had a large enclosed porch with many windows. No other home had the flowers we had. She would even wash, that is, spray the flowers, taking a mouthful of water and spraying it on them. The success with flowers was possibly due to the rain-water we used, which we carried from the cistern not far away, next to the church. When I think of it, I still feel the weight on my hands from carrying so much water just to make the flowers grow. The whole village admired the beautiful variety of flowers, which pleased me too.

While the children of the teacher-family easily became part of the community and its youth, there were not many in the village of the same educational standing for our parents to associate with on the same basis. The nearest village to Johannestal was Neusatz, a much smaller village, but with a teacher-family, very close to ours. The name of the teacher-family was Stuhlfeier and our visits with them were many.

Chapter 4
VILLAGE EDUCATION

It was the very nature of Russia German people to press education, however meager, wherever they moved to. This I found not only in Russia, but later also in Argentina and Brazil, which I will point out in a later chapter.

A church in a village also meant a school for the children in the village. And, school for the children also meant religious training for the entire youth of the village. The school principal, therefore, had to be qualified to play the church organ, know his Bible, to teach it sincerely, and to fulfill many of the pastor's duties, which was the case in a parish of more than one village. The teacher had to give special religious instructions to the members of the confirmation class and prepare them for confirmation. Confirmation usually took place on Palm Sunday. The catechism was the textbook, and that catechism had to be memorized, so that on examination day the communicant was able to answer the questions put to him. On confirmation day, the confirmand took his first communion and was looked upon as a person with special standing.

The local teacher, thus, had a great responsibility in the community. A few years before my exit from Russia, the new ruling of the government was that every German village was to have a resident Russian teacher to teach in Russian so that the pupils might be indoctrinated in the affairs of the government. I feel this was a good move on the part of the government. Another good innovation was to place a nurse in the village, supported by the government. Grossliebental, a much larger village, had a doctor. There were no charges for visits.

I remember very well when the first Russian teacher was assigned to Johannestal. It was in 1910. He was very well received by the community, and the children benefited from his presence in many ways. The village education was entirely supported by the community—no government subsidy. The families of the community contributed alike to the school needs.

It might be of interest to note that the teachers were all strict disciplinarians, using the rod, not only on the backs of the youngsters, but also on the palm of the hands. Sometimes when the teacher was too severe, the parent would show up and speak his mind in not too complimentary terms. But, in general, the parents cooperated very well with the teachers.

In the teaching plan, the Bible history lesson was always the first hour in the morning, alternating with the two Testaments.

A classroom system, arranging or seating the pupils according to their learning efforts, the best pupils to the front and the poorer student to the rear, I feel, was not an encouragement to better study. Another disadvantage was the long pews, with too many seated in one pew, thus encouraging restlessness and disturbing one another. The classes were large in number, as many as forty and fifty in a class. It is evident that with the above facts and disadvantages, the whole school system left much to be desired. In larger villages with more educated people, the school system took on a much better picture.

Chapter 5
MY HIGH SCHOOL YEARS AWAY FROM HOME

To attend high school meant leaving Johannestal where we lived and going to Grossliebental. First, it was my brother Viktor and now it was my turn. Viktor, after finishing Zentral-Schule, stayed to take a course in bookkeeping in Odessa. After he finished his course, he found immediate employment in Odessa as a bookkeeper.

My mother had a brother and a sister living in Grossliebental. I stayed with my uncle the first year, but the second year I moved into the school dormitory. The third year, I was home with the family, who had since moved to Grossliebental, leaving father in Johannestal to take care of his duties there.

The first year in high school meant getting adjusted to many things all new to me. It meant living with other young men in the same dorm and especially following strict rules of the school, such as conduct in the school building and outside in the view of the public. This school was the alma mater of both my father and my brother which, in itself, meant that infractions on my part would reflect upon my father and brother.

The students of this school were very close to one another. They were together nearly every day of the week, including Sunday in church.

The main subjects taught were: history, geography, mathematics, geometry, physics, Russian and German, drawing, music and carpentry. The first thing on the schedule was assembly (standing up), led by the teacher of German.

My greatest surprise in this school came at the end of the school term with the announcement of the nature of the final examination. Take, for example, the course in history. The textbook was divided into as many sections as there were students in the class, every section numbered and the students were informed of the sections. On the day of examination, all students appeared in the classroom. In front of the room was a long table with two or three teachers seated behind it. On the side wall was placed a bench that could seat three men. On the long table with the teachers behind, was a box that contained the numbers and the titles of the sections. The first student who came forth was asked to reach into the box and pick a number, and then asked to sit on the side bench to think about his subject. Then the second student was called to come forth and pick a number and to sit down to think about his number and the lesson. After the third student had picked his number, the first-number student came to appear before the teachers and, without being questioned, recited his lesson. If he was unable to go on, questions would be asked about the lesson and when his time was up, he was asked to leave the room. It is quite evident that, with a system of this kind, there was no chance to cheat.

The music students (and that meant the majority of us) had to be able to play all the church hymns and were examined every week by the teacher. If he knew his lesson, the next assignment was given. It was mandatory that every student who expected to become a teacher be able to play the organ. That was as essential as the knowledge of any other subject. He also had to be proficient in both Russian and German.

Manual training was also mandatory for every student. The school had a large room for this training, with all the necessary equipment, such as tables and tools. Some of the finest woods were here in abundant supply. The students taking manual training really looked forward to being able to work in the shop. Some of the finest work was turned out at this shop, and the students took home their work with visible pride.

The students of this school wore uniforms (not military), in school and out of school, thus making them stand out in public. Needless to say, the students wore their uniforms with justifiable pride. They were looked up to in the community, and they knew it.

I left this school in 1914 for reasons that I will explain later. Another student, after graduating from this Zentral-Schule, went to the United States to pursue his studies and to prepare himself for the ministry of the gospel. He was from the nearby village of Neuburg. He, too, had relatives in the United States who helped him financially upon arrival and in the subsequent years of further studies for the ministry. His name was Jacob Hirning, a young man of exceptional intelligence. Mr. Hirning was in his last year and I in the first in the Zentral-Schule. I had not heard from him until the rumors were circulated that Mr. Hirning was coming back to visit his parents and to claim his bride. The announcement was also made that Mr. Hirning would be speaking in the grammar school hall. What happened after his arrival and subsequently after his talk, I will relate in the next chapter.

Chapter 6
A SCHOOLMATE RETURNS FROM AMERICA

At the indicated time and place of the meeting to hear Reverend Jacob Hirning, my mother and I got ready to be there in plenty of time. The hall was filled with guests, numbering in the hundreds, because all wanted to hear a local boy who had made good. He was known also by his pastor when he attended the Zentral-Schule in Grossliebental. In fact, the pastor introduced him to us, indicating that Mr. Hirning had been ordained into the ministry by the Congregational Church in the United States. We were held captive by his ability to speak, and with what he had to say. He spoke of how he had left Russia and finally become convinced that he should enter the ministry.

After the meeting, many questions were directed to him, and an opportunity was given to many to talk to him. Mother and I too met him face to face, asking about life in the States. Everyone went away from this meeting feeling it was a blessing to hear this minister, a son from our midst who had made good.

At home, mother and I had a long talk, deep into the night, about my future. Her deepest yearning had always been that I, too, should choose the ministry as my calling. Mother mentioned how much she had prayed of late that her wish for me might come true. But, this night I could read her face and tell from her words how much she meant it.

I had no special reason to not fulfill her wishes. In our family and in the circles of our pietistic members, to go into the ministry always meant, "Did you receive a call?" "Has God called you into the ministry?" In the terms of my family and those of our friends, I was not yet converted. Mother felt that I should go to America and with our prayers what must be done would happen. I had no objection to this and hoped secretly it might become possible. We knelt down to pray, and never in all the prayers I heard coming from her lips, have I heard a prayer so sincere, so full of deep emotion and tears, as this prayer. After her prayer, we both felt a sense of relief and joy, knowing now something good would happen.

We both looked ahead now, far away to America, the land of freedom and endless possibilities. Mother wrote to her brother, John Riegel, in Willa (near Hebron), North Dakota, that I would be coming and should be received like a son.

The next step was to hasten my getting ready, to be able to leave when Reverend Hirning and his wife would be leaving. This was not as easy as it appeared. There was the matter of a passport, but for that, the time was too short. If I wanted to leave with the Hirnings, I would have to go minus a passport.

Facts were current that untold numbers would simply go in hopes of crossing the border into Poland with the help of agents by paying them a certain sum of money, for which they would guide us, by night, across the border. The road to cross the border often meant going through corn fields, over streams, and through dangerous swamps. To evade the customs officers, one had to get off the train station before the border where the agents would be readily available.

I decided to get ready and leave when the Hirnings left. We boarded the train together and, on the train, were assigned a cabin for four. But, there were only three of us, short one.

With money, in Russia, anything was possible. When the conductor came around checking on the railroad tickets, he noticed that here was room for still another passenger. We tipped him liberally and he forthwith placed the shingle above the cabin—"filled." We were happy to be just the three of us.

The train trip took a few days and nights. With this newlywed couple in the cabin, cooing and making endless endearing remarks to one another, I wished I had been with the rest of the passengers in the cars.

All went well, however, until, to the surprise and astonishment of all three of us, the border officials, instead of boarding the train at the last station, appeared two stations ahead of the border. The Hirnings had their passports, but I sat there dumbfounded, not knowing what to do.

An officer in civilian clothes came and asked me to come along with him leaving the train. The Hirnings, having a pass, drove on and I did not see them anymore until much later—in the States.

The officer took me to the police station, where I was interrogated, with the result that I was put into jail and my suitcase (a reed basket) thrown down a basement. If ever I thought hard and long of my God and my mother, it was here. Two others were with me in the jail. No one talked and no smiles greeted me. The room was dark. In the room, filthy and smelly, in the corner, was a pail of water. I faced the wall, and if I ever prayed with the deepest of feeling, it was here. My faith, however, was still with me. I knew God would somehow bring me out of this dungeon.

After spending one night in the jail, no bed, and on the hard floor, the next day early a guard came, calling me to come to the office. When I was interrogated the day before, I had to surrender my money and other items I had on my person. Knowing that I had a little money, the officer asked me if I would be willing to be taken back to Odessa accompanied by a civilian guard rather than by a uniformed police officer. I said I would gladly pay to be taken to Odessa as a "free" prisoner.

The next day, we took the train back to Odessa and went straight to police headquarters. The first officer I met was the one who had turned down my application for a passport, saying it was impossible to issue one to go with the Hirnings. He smiled at me sarcastically, saying, "Aha, you did not want to wait." I asked for permission to call my cousin, a medical doctor, stationed at Odessa Evangelical Hospital, telling him to come and help me in my problem. I called him and, in twenty minutes, he arrived. Dr. Gottlieb Gross had a good reputation as a doctor in Odessa and was well-known. When he came, we shook hands and I told him my story. He went to the desk and asked the officer to see the chief. In a minute, the desk officer came back and said to the doctor: "Poschalusty v pristutsvie," meaning, "Please, come to his presence."

It took only ten minutes. When the doctor came out from the chief's office, he said to me, "You are free." Right then and there, I applied for a passport and was granted it before leaving the headquarters. I thanked my cousin profusely and proceeded to go back home to Grossliebental where mother and the children lived. It took just a few days to get ready again, this time adding a few more things to take along to America.

Father had come to visit and to help me get everything in order and then went back to his work. The day to leave came. Mother, my younger brother and I, drove by team to Odessa. The parting was very sad. But, amid the sorrow of parting, there was an inner feeling, "it is God's will." I took the train to Libau and, from there, the ship *Roccia* to Halifax, Canada. From Canada I went to Chicago and then to Hebron, North Dakota.

On the ship, I had a second-class cabin with three others in my room. Most passengers from Russia and other countries seeking the promised land, went third class. Otherwise a strong and robust man, full of courage, I am a weakling on board a ship. For three days and nights, I was sea-sick, eating only a little cheese and onions. The captain of the ship would come down and say, "Do you want to spend eternity in your room? Come up on deck." After three days, I began to eat. Otherwise, the period in the ship was not very eventful, except for the treatment the third-class passengers received from the sailors, and the young girls who were forever pursued and taken advantage of.

The train trip to Hebron, North Dakota, too, was uneventful. Most of the passengers were foreigners, representing many countries, and who got off the train at different points along the way. Some of us could talk with one another in European languages, but none of us knew English. So far, all the English I knew, was "Mr." On the train, many of us picked up a few words and sentences from the interpreter who was with us.

It was Pentecost of 1914 when I arrived at Hebron, North Dakota. Being Sunday, many people had gathered at the station, awaiting the arrival of the train to see who would get off and on. Coming closer and closer to Hebron, I pondered, "What will happen when I get there?" My uncle Riegel knew I was coming, but did not know my day of arrival. "Will I know anyone? Where can I go? I don't know the language and the town is totally strange to me!" But, my spirits were high, for I was now in the United States.

The train stopped. Taking my reed-basket of belongings, I arose and, as I looked out of the car window, I saw a multitude of people milling outside on the platform of the station. My heart became heavy. Was it fear? Not exactly; maybe it was anxiety about the unknown. As I came to the steps of the train to step down, my eyes dropped. What next? I began to walk into the crowd, feeling,

I am a total stranger, no one knows me. But I hoped for the best. Suddenly, I raised my head and what did I see? One, two, three young men I knew in the village of Johannestal. Was it really true, or had the long trip dazed me? No, it was a reality. I called them by name and when they noticed me, they called me by my first name. I set my suitcase down and all eyes rested on me. In the next few minutes, about fifteen young people, all from Johannestal, where we lived for many years, gathered around me to greet me. I was invited by a young Fischer boy to come to his home. My joy was great! A man just now from Russia! The evening in the Fischer home was a long-remembered one. Dozens of German townspeople came and filled the home. The conversation lasted late into the night. So many questions had to be answered. Also, questions were asked about the present attitude of the Russian government toward the German people in Russia.

The next day, Uncle Riegel showed up in Hebron. I asked him, after a happy greeting, how he knew I was there. He said he had a feeling I would be there. Business reasons also necessitated his coming to Hebron, so, even if I had not come, the trip would not have been in vain.

I remembered my uncle only faintly. He had left for the States because of a broken love affair. He settled about twenty miles south of Hebron, where he homesteaded. He was now married and had two children.

On the way to Willa from Hebron, we had plenty of time to talk, undisturbed, and recall special events and people in Grossliebental. Arriving at Willa, a town with just a store and a post office, I had another pleasant surprise. The storekeeper, Mr. Heinle, approached and, when he saw me, exclaimed, "Willy Gross, from Johannestal!" I recognized him too, for he had been a substitute teacher in our village. He insisted on having me step down, meet his wife and daughters and have a cup of coffee. It was now getting toward evening and time to drive on, but many times in the future did I find my way here to the Heinles, not too far from my new home.

I stayed with my uncle on the farm and got acquainted with the American way of farming. I stayed there until late fall, helping with harvesting, threshing and fall plowing.

My uncle belonged to the Congregational Church, just a few

miles from the farm. Here I met many German people and, surprisingly again, most of them from Johannestal. I liked the informality and the freedom of the church. Occasionally, college students would come for a visit, and getting acquainted with them pleased me very much.

I stayed with Uncle Riegel until fall, when I went to Bowdle, South Dakota, to the uncles from Father's side. I was now introduced to a type of farming totally unfamiliar to me. The plowing here was not walking alongside or behind the plow, but sitting on the plow and regulating it at times from that position.

My uncle had a number of quarters of land, much of which was still virgin prairie. The first crop on virgin soil was usually flax. Flax needed good soil and it also brought a good price.

What I had never experienced in Russia was rocky soil. The land of my uncle, however, was full of rocks, which made plowing a problem, both from the standpoint of security on the plow and also from the standpoint of untrained horses running away and dragging you along. The number of times I fell off the plow I am ashamed to admit. Luckily, the horses were trained and never ran away on me.

The harvesting season, my first in this country, was a real joy to me. The new type of harvesting, with the cut grain elevated into the header-box was, for me, a thrill to watch. The many stacks of grain on the fields, in even numbers, was a picture I shall never forget. In the old country, the grain was hauled into the village, a long and time-consuming process, requiring many teams and men to help.

The threshing season was new to me, too. In the old country, with their set-up, dozens of people were required to take care of every phase of threshing; pitching grain into the separator, filling the sacks of clean grain, hauling away the straw and the chaff, and so on. Here, threshing was a chore requiring only a few people. Having worked on the farm a number of summers myself, I found out that the threshing season is no easy task for those who are on top of stacks, pitching bundles or loose grain, day after day.

With two uncles from Father's side living six miles out of Bowdle, South Dakota, I agreed with Uncle Riegel that I might visit with them also. I left in the fall and stayed with Uncle Christian for a year, helping with many farm chores. He was a large-scale farmer for those days, with many cows, horses and other farm life. Uncle Gross had six children, two boys and four girls, but at home on the farm were a son and three daughters.

In the winter, cousin John would take care of the horses and I took care of the cows. We enjoyed each other's company and had a real good time. This family was a congenial and peace-loving group of people. The other uncle, Jacob, lived only half a mile away. The visits there were many, but I never stayed there any length of time.

Here at Bowdle with my uncle, I began seriously to learn the English language. Uncle's youngest daughter, Emma, was daily going to grade school two miles away, a country school. The teacher, Mr. Adam Eisenmann, also of German background and still able to speak German, was the teacher. I asked to be enrolled and was gladly accepted. The teacher was kind and patient with me, giving me extra time to learn the English language.

Staying in Bowdle for about two years, I also got acquainted with the Congregational Church. Both of my uncles in Bowdle attended the Congregational Church. The greatest help that came to me from the standpoint of the future of my calling, came from the pastor of the local church, Reverend G. L. Brakemeyer, who lived in Bowdle. He took special interest in me, guiding me in a fatherly way as the feeling in me to become a minister grew faster and faster. He would tell me all about the church in this land. To him, I owe my final decision to enter Redfield College.

Chapter 7
THE TURNING POINT IN MY LIFE

My parents always stressed education and hard work to finally be a success. Again and again, mother would say, "Education no one can take from you and hard physical work will be a credit in time of need." I always did enjoy physical labor, possibly more than hard mental work. Being on my own in this new country, I knew that in order to be able to go on to school, I would need to use physical labor to gain the financial means to go through the many required years of advanced schooling.

During my first summer in America, I hired out to work in the threshing season, pitching bundles and loose grain. Many mornings upon rising, I could hardly open my hand to wash myself. Only determination and my life's objectives would enable me to persevere. I never gave up this hard work until I moved to Bowdle, South Dakota. Here too, I worked hard for my second cousin, a businessman living in town; I lived in the vacant house on the farm, cooked for myself, did my own washing, took charge of the cows, horses and whatever chores were necessary on the farm. Possibly the hardest work for me on this farm was husking corn. My still somewhat tender hands often bled from the sharp corn husks. In time of temptations to take it easy, my objective would always appear before me.

I was happy, however, when Sunday came. Attending church on Sunday was always uppermost in my mind. Meeting people, old and young, and talking to the pastor, were my greatest joys. The pastor would go out of his way to take extra time to talk about my future. He would stress the need to attend our College, Redfield, South Dakota. The school in Redfield was a combination college and seminary. Attendance there was the first step toward attaining my goal.

Chapter 8
THE YEARS IN REDFIELD COLLEGE, REDFIELD, SOUTH DAKOTA

Redfield College Seminary was financed and maintained by the German branch of the Congregational Church. Most of the students came from the rural areas. The college was coeducational, and married students were also admitted. The enrollment was small, never more than three hundred. There were two main buildings on the rather large campus. A number of residences were off the campus, one of which was the girls' dormitory, about a block away from the main buildings. The president and all the teachers, except the teacher of English, could also understand the German language. German was essential, because preaching in our churches was, at this time, all in the German language.

Many students had to work in the college and outside to supplement money from home and the money earned in the summer. Being one of those who needed financial aid, I wrote to the school for possible help, sending along with my application a recommendation from Reverend Brakemeyer. In just a few days, a letter came with the promise of financial help. What a lift this gave me! At last, I was accepted in the school where my secret desire, to study for the ministry, would come true.

Upon arrival at Redfield College, my dormitory quarters were assigned to me, and my job, taking care of the third-story floor, was described to me. I had to clean the rooms and make and change the beds. For this, I would get free quarters and a promise of a better-paying job the following year.

Things went very well. Most of the subjects were in the German language, but English gave me trouble. I made it a practice to memorize twenty new words a day. My English books had many German words written above, and vice versa. Possibly the hardest task was to make my English sound English. The English language is harder than many want to believe. There is too much to guess and too much just to memorize. But, I had to know the language and learn it fast.

The second year in Redfield was easier, both language-wise and especially financially. During the summer, I earned well on the farm and, returning to school, I was elected manager of the Boarding Club, thus earning my board, plus twenty-five dollars a month. As manager, I had to maintain two cows, buy hay for them, buy the necessary groceries for the kitchens, and hire the cook and waitresses. For two years, I had this job and was able to run it so well that, at the end of the year, every student was able to get a refund.

There was a good spirit among the students, as well as a good teacher-student relationship. With the smaller classrooms, every student had access to the teacher. With the small enrollment and the limited number of teachers, not to speak of the shortage of finances, athletics was confined to basketball only. There was a tennis court that many used, but the interest of all the students was in basketball. We had no coach. Sometimes a coach from a downtown high school would come to help us, or a teacher who might have been a basketball player in earlier years would help us out. Most of the coaching was done by ourselves. Our gym was small, not according to regulations, but we did a lot of practicing in it. Whenever we played a competitive team, we would use a downtown gym. I must say, we had one of the best teams in the state.

All students were expected to attend the morning worship on Sunday at eleven o'clock. One of the preacher-teachers would give the sermon. Late afternoons on Sunday, the young people met as a *Schiller-Club*, a program which consisted of brief scriptural talks, singing, debates, and essays.

After supper, the students were free to attend any youth group or church downtown, but had to be in their rooms by ten o'clock at night.

In the wintertime, the school held two weeks of nightly evangelistic meetings, conducted by a minister of our denomination. These meetings were conducted in conformity with our pietistic background, where persons would seek a personal commitment to Christ. Many students would thank this school for the new spiritual life found in the chapel of Redfield College. The turning point, as far as making the experience of a personal commitment of my life to Christ and his ministry, came here at the college. From now on, I was fully determined to reach my goal. The "call" into the ministry was no more a question, but a reality!

I corresponded regularly with my parents up to now. At times, they would refer to rumors of war that would involve the United States too. They, of course, were already at war. Mother was most anxious about the future of all of us, but their future looked very dark to them. Even though Mother was glad to see me go to America, she was, nevertheless, anxious, because I was the only one missing in the family. In one of her letters, she wrote that she prayed to God, "Why did my son have to go to America?" The answer to her prayer came, "What I am doing now you will find out later."

Chapter 9

A YEAR IN MILITARY SERVICE

As this country was at war with Germany, many of our men were drafted into service. Redfield College had about a dozen eligible men to be drawn into military service, most of them seminary students. Most of the men, however, registered in their home towns. Three of us, thinking it would not make any difference to register at home or at Redfield, registered locally. When America entered the war against Germany, the feeling toward the college changed radically. We were looked upon as "pro-German," a feeling which was absolutely false. Every effort on our part could not change this feeling against us. Rumors were rampant that certain elements in the community planned to blow up the college. Only through the intervention of the local bank, whose president was on our school board, was the tragedy prevented.

On the local draft board was an attorney, Mr. Bull, who was the epitome of the hatred against us, and saw to it that the three of us who registered locally were immediately drafted into service. The difference between the three of us was the fact that I was the only one not yet a citizen. I had taken the first papers shortly after I came to this country in Hettinger County, Mott, North Dakota.

As a seminary student, I could have claimed exemption, but did not do so. On June 20, 1918, I entered the service, destination, Camp Funston, Kansas, Company H, 20th Infantry. I was not the only one not a citizen drafted into military service. Upon arriving at Fort Riley, Kansas, there must have been two hundred of us, standing all in one group, hearing the question whether we wanted to become citizens of the United States. Without exception, all of us answered in the affirmative. I was now proud to be a citizen of this country. In peacetime, I would have had to wait another year to get my second papers. The training at Camp Funston was strenuous, especially the long marches with heavy packs on our backs. One such long march I will never forget: it was a thirty-mile march. Many fell out and had to be picked up by the ambulance following the marching soldiers. It was really hot on this march and perspiration was so intense that, in my case at least, it oozed through the wrapped-around leggings. I am proud to say that I made every lengthy march without dropping out of the ranks.

The most pleasant thing about all the marches was that, when we marched into the camp at eveningtime, the band would usually meet us at the edge of town and lead us home with marching music. How soothing it was to feel our legs becoming increasingly lighter.

Strange as it may seem, the regulation rifle, used every day, became attached to me, or I to it. I wished I could have taken it home with me when I was discharged.

A few months after the war, I was transferred to Fort Benjamin Harrison, Indianapolis, Indiana. No more strenuous daily exercise was necessary. Preliminary announcements were made that in a month we would all be shipped to France. Preparations to leave had already been completed when the report came that the war had ended, and that we would stay where we were.

From then on, more and more of the soldiers were discharged. I patiently waited for my name to come up, but it still took some time. The daily training became less and less. In fact, the captain one day asked for private secretaries in his office. Such men were few, most of them having been discharged. I volunteered and was accepted. From this time on, my life in the army was a matter of passing time and waiting for the discharge. That day, June 10, 1919, came and the discharge took place in Camp Dodge, Iowa, where most of the boys were finally discharged.

Military service was not unfamiliar to me, for marching and discipline I knew in Russia, not as a soldier, but as a student.

For me, military life was not a burden. It had to be done and, after all, I was an American now. On Sunday, when not on duty, I would go into the city of Indianapolis, looking up churches and settling on one to attend. To my great surprise, I found a German Methodist Church, attended it and enjoyed it very much. Sometimes, people would invite me for dinner or some social function of the church. In camp, I spent hours in YMCA's, reading and taking home with me the variety of literature on the racks.

I must confess that I did not get any further in the Army than the rank of first-class private. Many times, I would ask myself, why? The only answer that I could come up with was that my German background had something to do with it, or very likely that Mr. Bull of the draft board at Redfield might have transferred his hatred to headquarters. My reputation in the army was good and my conduct was flawless. The top sergeant often remarked that I should be a corporal or a sergeant. However, I made the best of the situation.

First school I attended in the United States, in 1915, six miles south of Bowdle, South Dakota.

Chapter 10
BACK TO REDFIELD COLLEGE

With no immediate relatives to come back to upon my discharge, I couldn't decide to which uncle in South and North Dakota I would go. I first visited them all, including my girlfriend of college days, who lived in Coleharbor, North Dakota. The visiting time was brief in each place. With the harvest time and the threshing season to follow, I needed to go to work again. The work was hard, but the earnings were good. In the fall, I returned for my remaining two years at Redfield College.

These last two years in the college-seminary were very happy years. To begin with, I had earned well during the summer and, with the savings while in the army, the year ahead looked good to me. During the summer of the last two years, the theology students did summer preaching, usually in vacant or small churches. My two last summers were spent in Isabel, South Dakota. There was an English Congregational church in Isabel and a German one that was still unable to have a permanent minister. The congregation was small in number and the building was an old vacated lumber building with a high front. I lived upstairs in this building and did my own cooking to save money. At times, I would go to the restaurant for a square meal, or accept an invitation from one of the members. All members lived in the country and I did not have any means of transportation. On Sunday mornings when the people came to church, or quite frequently during the week, many of the ladies of the church would bring me food and special delectables they knew I liked.

The second summer in Isabel was especially interesting. I bought my first car, a Model T Ford. Needless to say, I felt I preached better after the purchase of a car. I already knew how to drive, and no driver's tests were taken in those days. Now, with a car, I could make visits and expand my summer preaching field. Two more outpost people approached me about starting Sunday Schools in their areas. It did not take very long before these country places were weekly increasing in number. The Sunday schools were on Sunday nights and week nights. Whenever I had a Sunday night free, I would attend the English Congregational Church.

Being proud to own a car, I could allow myself a longer trip now and then. To drive to North Dakota where Uncle Riegel lived would take a little over half a day.

The trip took me through an Indian reservation, poor roads, sand and deep ruts that often blocked the car. I felt the going somewhat heavy and soon got into deep sand. The car, not being new, but one that had gone through many rough roads, I trusted. I hoped all would be well. But, not so. The car stalled. What was the matter? The motor was running, but not the car. The axle was broken. Now, what to do? I was miles from the nearest town. In the distance, I saw a farmhouse; maybe there I could find help.

Walking about two miles, I saw it appeared to be an Indian home, and so it was. Only children and a squaw sitting on the floor were to be seen. It took a long time for them to understand what I wanted. Finally, the man of the house arrived and I was able to make him understand what I wanted. I wanted to have him pull me out of the sand and, if possible, pull me to the next town, and was willing to pay him liberally.

All of my pleading and coaxing were in vain. He said he just could not do it, giving no specific reason. He had both a car and a tractor on his place.

I went back to my Ford and just waited and hoped for the best. It paid off. Another car came and I asked him to pull me to the nearest town. He complied. It cost me sixteen dollars, but I would have been willing to pay much more, for it was about twenty miles to the nearest town. The name of the town was McIntosh. Here I left my car to be repaired, stating that I would be back in three days. I took the train the rest of the way to see my uncle. When I returned, the car was ready and I arrived back in Isabel without any further mishaps.

Another interesting event took place one afternoon when an Indian on horseback came to my door begging for a loan of twenty-five dollars until he came back from an Indian "pow wow" fifteen miles away. To reenforce his pleas, he said he belonged to another Indian reservation where Reverend Hertz was the missionary. I knew Reverend Hertz. Having pity on the young Indian, I yielded and gave him fifteen dollars. Well, I am still waiting!

It was always a joy to come back to school and relate the summer experiences. The schoolteachers were interested, of course, in how well we did in the summer, how much preaching and teaching we did, and how the people responded.

My last year in Redfield Seminary came to a close. I looked forward toward the ordination, the high point of all these years. Instead of accepting a call from a church, I chose, however, to go on to another college.

Chapter 11

MY ORDINATION

The German Congregational churches had their own conference, in the German language. The South Dakota State Conference met at Scotland, in a church in the country. To the churches in those days, inviting a conference meant furnishing free lodging and meals. The attendance was in the hundreds, with not only guests, but open to anyone who could attend.

At this conference, it was announced beforehand that five candidates for the ministry would be ordained. These candidates were: John P. Flemmer, Carl Green, Reinhold Knaus, Carl Schatz and myself.

The ordination took place after a sermon by a conference pastor. The candidates were examined one by one, each first giving a statement of his life and religious experiences, as well as a statement of his faith. Thereupon, after all interrogation had ended, the act of ordination took place. The candidates all knelt before the altar and, with the hands of the ministers laid upon them, the ordination prayer was spoken. It was always a solemn occasion. After the charge to the pastor and to the church were given, the new ministers were received by the conference guests.

This ordination, June 10, 1922, in Scotland, South Dakota, will remain forever the high point of my life. He who has not experienced such an occasion will have difficulty understanding it.

To my sorrow, I must indicate that I am the only one left alive of this group of five ordained on that day. All four made good in the ministry. They were faithful to their Master and to the churches that they served.

F. W. Gross, the soldier, 1918-1919.

Chapter 12

TWO YEARS IN CARLETON COLLEGE, NORTHFIELD, MINNESOTA

Dr. E. A. Fath, an alumnus of Carleton College was, for a few years, president of Redfield College. I had a long talk with him about going on with my education. He encouraged me to do so and suggested his alma mater. If I would go there, he said, I would choose one of the best schools. That I later found out to be true. The college is a grade-A institution and restricts its attendance. The students are mostly from upper economic level homes.

Dr. Fath taught astronomy and trigonometry upon returning to teaching. To attend a high-standard college required more money, which was not in abundance with me. But, I decided to enter Carleton and sent in my credits from Redfield, for which I was allowed two years of college credit. I entered as a junior. To make the further two more years a possibility, Dr. Fath, whose father was a Congregational minister, and who, with his wife, also lived in Northfield, promised me free lodging in the home of his parents. In turn, I would have to take care of the lawn and change the storm windows and screens when the time came to change them. This helped some, but was not enough to carry me through. Dr. Fath was also instrumental in securing a scholarship for me. In addition, the Minnesota Conference offered me a small church in Glencoe to serve every Sunday. This meant leaving for the church on Saturdays and staying the night at Glencoe to be able to preach at the morning service. The return to Northfield I was able to make on Sunday afternoon.

With this arrangement and the scholarship, I saw my way through financially. It was my strong ambition to join football, but with the arrangement of serving the church, football was out of the question. Since every student had to take some sport, I chose wrestling. I liked it. The discipline was hard. Certain foods had to be avoided. I became the recipient of the golden medal for the heavyweight championship in 1924.

The two years in Carleton College were happy years. Teachers like Dr. Fath, Dr. Vernon, Dr. Boodine, Dr. Vestling, and President Cowling, rated very high with me in Northfield.

The daily assemblies in Skinner Memorial Chapel were events of great importance. There were devotionals, outside speakers, and special music of the highest caliber. One speaker, William Jennings Bryan, I will never forget. After his address, the students asked many questions. The answer to one special question I still remember. A student asked Mr. Bryan what it was that had made him the public speaker he became. He answered: "If you have something to say, people will listen to you."

The Sunday night vesper services were attended also by people of the community. Skinner Memorial Chapel had a large pipe organ and a seating capacity of five hundred. It was noted for its beauty and location in the park or campus of the school.

Carleton was noted for its high degree of scholastic accomplishment, its debates, its orchestra and its choir. The student body consisted of many students from many states and countries. I think back on Carleton College with many pleasant memories.

Chapter 13
MARRIAGE AND THE TRIP TO CANADA

Graduating from Carleton College in 1924 also meant having a permanent pastorate. Among the many fields vacant in the States and in Canada, I chose Canada. My parish consisted of six churches, all churches in the country, and the parsonage in the country as well.

There was much work left to do before the graduation and immediately after the graduation. I needed a car to make the trip to Canada. The car problem was quickly settled. Dr. Fath sold me his Model T Ford. A trailer for the many items like books, dishes, and clothing was also bought in a short time.

The important event—getting married—and the work before and after, called for all the inner fortitude that we had.

Emilie is the fourth eldest of a family of nine children. Her parents, too, were born in Russia, the father from Rosenfelt and the mother, Elizabeth Schneider, from Neuburg, near Odessa. They came to this country in 1901 and settled on a farm in Coleharbor, North Dakota, where the family grew up. Mr. Bastian was a successful farmer and became a well-thought-of man in the community. Originally Lutheran, but later joining the Congregational Church, he became an influential man in our German Congregational Church. At one time, he was trustee of Redfield College and worked in a close relationship with the then president of Redfield College, Dr. E. A. Fath. The whole Bastian family was a strongly church-oriented family and remained so in the many years that followed.

Two of the daughters, Emilie and Lydia, went into the teaching profession, spending many years teaching at various schools, mostly in the Dakotas. Emilie attended Redfield College for a number of years and there I became acquainted with her. Later, she attended Dickinson College and also Valley City College, both colleges in North Dakota. In later years, the children became scattered, like many children of older families, seeking occupations and work in other states. Mr. and Mrs. Bastian spent their retirement years in Turtle Lake, North Dakota.

My bride had been teaching for four years and was now home with her parents. After school, I loaded up my belongings and drove to Coleharbor, North Dakota, where we had planned to become married at noon, June 19, 1924, in the little country church of Emilie Bastian, who was to become my wife.

The officiating pastor was Dr. J. L. Hirning, who was our teacher in Redfield College. The wedding guests were to be at the church by noon. Emilie's brother, Fred, was to meet Dr. Hirning at the railroad station. During the night, a torrential rain washed out the railroad and Dr. Hirning could not be met at the station. At home, we did not know why the minister was late. So, Emilie's father and I, with Mr. Bastian's Willys Knight, started out to meet Dr. Hirning and Emilie's brother, Fred. It took us only about three miles, till we sank into axle-deep mud. Now what? There was a farmer nearby to whom we went for help to get us out of the mire. His answer was, "If you unload my wagon, I will get a team of horses and with this wagon I will pull you out." His wagon was piled full of rocks. There was nothing else left to do but unload the heavy rocks. In the meantime, Fred had come back with the news that the train was not running and that the guests already at the church should be asked to go home. Mr. Bastian and I came back too, disappointed and at a loss of what to do next. We just sat, wondered and waited, hoping that something would take place.

To our great surprise and joy at 9:00 P.M., Dr. Hirning appeared with a car. Quickly the guests were notified that the wedding would take place at 10 P.M., and so it did. What a start, we said to each other! The bridal flowers that were ordered from Bismarck arrived the next day.

The following day, we loaded up our belongings on the car and trailer and started west, as far as Hebron, North Dakota. Developing a weak trailer hitch that connected the car, we spent some time with the blacksmith. That item fixed, we headed for La Havre, Montana and from there across the border to Mennyberries, Canada. Now in Canada, but not yet at Medicine Hat and Hilda, the final goal, we drove on more hopefully. The country was bare and uninviting. Not many cars or other vehicles met or passed us. Several times before getting to Medicine Hat, we lost our trailer and one time it tipped upside down. A passing band of gypsies with wagons smiled as they came closer to us, but did not offer any help.

Finally, arriving at Medicine Hat, we stopped at the customs office to declare our belongings, and to make all matters worse, they charged us $140 duty on what we had: car, trailer and books. I knew that this was not according to law, but I held my peace, hoping to settle it later. A month or so later, I attended a meeting in Calgary, where I had an interview with a top customs official. After listening to my story, he said: "Take this pencil and paper and write down what I am citing to you, the page, the paragraph and the book, so and so, and present it to the customs officer in Medicine Hat and he will give you back the duty he charged." This I did, and my money was all refunded to me.

From Medicine Hat, we still had to drive sixty miles to Hilda, Alberta, and six more miles to the church and parsonage.

As no one knew the date of our arrival, there was no one there to greet and welcome us. The parsonage was open and we made ourselves at home. The home was a two-story frame building, and for a country place, quite adequate. The yard was large and had a garage and barn. Yes, there was an out-house, a very important little frame building. There was also a well, not very deep, and the water was raised with two buckets on a wheel.

The parsonage had three bedrooms and a heater, but no furniture as yet, only what we brought along: books, clothes and dishes. We had little money, not many clothes, enough dishes to feed a dozen people, but no beds, no chairs and no tables. We got a bed—we had to—but for the longest time, a washtub was our table and later the ironing board served as our eating table. In spite of all this poverty, we were rich in hope and love, knowing we were here for the Cause of Christ.

Chapter 14
TWO YEARS IN CANADA

We lived in the province of Alberta. One of the six churches was located in the province of Saskatchewan. Both provinces were called the prairie states. With six churches in the parish, it meant much driving, which in the winter caused many problems. The winters were very cold, with heavy snows to plow through. I was the only one in the parish with a car. To help myself when encountering a lot of snow, I equipped the car with a pulley for the rear wheel, a sturdy rope, an axle, a heavy hammer, a shovel and warm gloves. When I got stuck in the snow, I would drive the axle into the ground, attaching the rope to it and on the pulley, on the other end, thus pulling myself out of the snow in the winter and out of the mud at other times.

The people of my parish came originally from the Dakotas, seeking here a better life, or in some cases, escaping heavy indebtednesses or minor infractions of the law. The people were all poor. We soon realized the overwhelming problems we had to face, such as quarreling among themselves, where to get even the barest means of existence, because of crop failures, and how, in our own case, to get contributions to help sustain the pastor's financial needs.

As per arrangements, the Mission contributed the stipulated amount and the rest had to come from the parish members. What came in in a month from the people was practically nil.

We did not starve, however. With the consecutive crop failures, the farmers would butcher much of their stock. They would save as much as possible by processing it into sausages, smoking and freezing it in the winter. In spite of all this, there was much meat left over. The pastor's family was flooded with meat to the point that we did not know what to do with it. We could not refuse it, for fear of hurting the people's feelings. The only alternative was simply to bury it in the ground. But, even with the diminishing number of their stock, many of the farmers lost as many as ten heads just from starvation.

With repeated crop failures, the people had no financial income; consequently, the time came when they walked in rags. In the winter, this created the problem, especially, of shoes. How well I remember a neighboring little boy coming to the parsonage one day saying, "Pastor, may I have some shoes?" The toes of both feet were bare and, outside, the snow was four inches deep.

A month earlier, I wrote to the Women's Missionary Society about the plight of the people of my parish. Help came in two weeks—bales of clothing for distribution among the people. This was a great relief. From far and near, the people came to receive clothing and shoes. This assistance raised the spirit of the people, if only temporarily.

In their needs, the people would come to us for every kind of assistance. With no cars, they would come to me to take them to the doctor or to the hospital, which were sixty miles away in Medicine Hat. My neighbor came to me for a badly needed haircut (no long-haired people then). A woman came to have her glasses soldered. A man not far from the parsonage came, complaining about pains in his tummy. He did not want to go to the hospital. He hoped I would massage him, which I did. It helped temporarily, but soon, I was informed that he died. I realized I was not a good nurse.

Our financial needs were somewhat alleviated by a public-school teacher rooming with us. Her schoolhouse was a mile and a half from the parsonage. She walked to school and back every day. An amusing event to us, but not to her, took place one morning. The teacher had to leave early to get the room open and bring it into an orderly condition, for the inspector was to visit her school that day. In the winter, she had to have the schoolhouse comfortably heated. All this meant the teacher had to be in school long before nine o'clock.

On this particular morning, before leaving, she went, as she did many times before, to the outdoor rest room. This toilet had two hooks, one inside and one outside. Being already late, she hurried outside and to the rest room and quickly slammed the door, only to find that the outside hook closed her in. We were of the impression she had gone on to school until I went outside and heard a pounding on the rest room door. Quickly I opened the door and found her in bitter tears. "I am late to school," she said. Quickly I took my car and drove her to school. Many times later, all three of us laughed about this episode.

The greatest event so far in Canada, and in our lives, for that matter, was the arrival of our firstborn. Knowing the winter conditions in Canada and the long distance from our home to Medicine Hat to a hospital, we made early arrangements, both with the doctor and with one of our members to have a team of horses and a sled ready, in case we could not go by car. We thought our figuring was correct and had the doctor's word to substantiate the expected time of arrival of our child. But the calculations, both ours and the doctor's, were amiss. On a Thursday morning at ten o'clock, March 12, 1925, my wife informed me she was having labor pains. What? Ten days ahead of our calculation, and no time to lose! Quickly I notified my member with team of horses and the sled to come to drive to Medicine Hat. He had the horses in readiness. During the night, four inches of snow had fallen, so that the use of the car would be too great a risk. Even though it was the month of March, the weather was still bitter cold. In an hour, we were on our way. Mr. Miller, the owner of the team and the driver, my wife, in pain, packed into the sled, with a hot stone under her feet and bundled up to keep her as comfortable as possible, and I, started out on an unforgettable trip. The horses had long icicles suspended from their lips. A brief stop on the way at a farmhouse and a bite to eat helped immensely. A little relaxed, we drove on, for we were still a long way from Medicine Hat. Soon we noticed one of the horses slowing down. It was apparent that he would give out on us shortly. We were still more than halfway from our goal. The driving had to be slowed down to save the horse. To lighten the load with still about twelve miles to go, I got off the sled and walked the rest of the way beside the sled. The one horse practically pulled the whole load.

We arrived at the hospital at ten o'clock, after an eleven-hour trip. The next morning, our first child was born. What an experience! Our first child, a son, Vernon Quentin Gross, was healthy and strong, despite the harrowing trip.

In those days, a new mother had to stay in the hospital for as long as eleven days before she could leave. Our doctor was very kind and helpful, giving the mother many good suggestions on how to care for the child.

After eleven days, I took the car to bring my family home from Medicine Hat. There was very little snow, but the roads were open and one could make good time with the car. I stayed overnight in Medicine Hat, planning to return home the next day. During the night and the next morning, the chinook winds came, softening the frozen roads and melting the ice, so that the driving home by car became very difficult and prolonged, so much so that Mrs. Gross did not have enough milk to nurse the child. We stopped in a small country store to buy food and liquids to provide nourishment for the child. By the time we arrived home, it was one o'clock in the morning.

Church work consisted of preaching every Sunday, teaching Sunday school, holding prayer meetings, in some places confirmation school on Saturday, many counseling sessions, and settling quarrels between families about boundaries, fences and even going to court in some cases. One case especially aroused considerable fear in the church. A husky farmer in the community one afternoon, when he knew of a teenage girl home alone, entered her home and raped her. She was the organist of the local church. The case came before court, but with no witnesses, and the case was lost. The people of the community, always fearing this man, warned me, saying, "Pastor, look out, this man is very dangerous, he might kill you for taking a stand against him." I had no fear of him, nor did I, at any time, try to avoid facing him. He had a very good wife and his children were active in the church.

After two years in Canada, we felt it was time to move back to the States.

Chapter 15
BACK TO THE STATES—
MERRICOURT, NORTH DAKOTA

A call from the Merricourt parish was accepted with joy. Just two years in Canada was not a very good record for a young pastor with a lot of energy, but we felt justified to move under the trying circumstances.

Before going directly to Merricourt, we first went to Turtle Lake, North Dakota, to visit the in-laws and because we expected our second child any day.

I drove on to Merricourt to preach my first sermon. After the sermon, a boy at the door greeted me with a telegram that Grace was born, on July 4, 1926, in Washburn, North Dakota.

My father-in-law, as per plan, was to take my wife to Bismarck to the hospital for confinement, but the stork was faster than the car, so they had had to turn in at Washburn instead. All went well at the small hospital. In a few days, I drove up to get the family.

The Merricourt parish consisted of two churches, one in town and the other in the country, some twelve miles away. The members of the country church (Hoffnungsfeld) were all well-to-do, living on their own farms, growing grain and raising cattle. They were all good people and willing to make a success of the church.

The members in town were mostly retired members and a few business people. The church in town was new and so was the parsonage. The parsonage was owned by both churches. The town was small, with a population of only about two hundred. I served the churches alternately.

To develop a good spirit among the young and, at the same time, do something constructive, we met on a rotating basis in the farm homes once a week for discussion and to learn handiwork. In Carleton College, I had acquired the skill of basketry and raffia weaving. It was interesting to see the glow in the faces of the young people, sitting in a ring in the kitchen with a tub of reeds in the center, making baskets and weaving shopping and hand bags.

It was always the event to look forward to every week.

The country church also had a men's double quartet that met for practice every week. Rain or shine, summer or winter, plowing time or harvest time, this double quartet would meet regularly. They loved to sing, and they did well, too. They were frequently invited to sing for special occasions. There was much more activity in the country church than in the town church. The town church did not have the young or the middle-aged elements to become more active.

Not having too much to do in this field and becoming somewhat restless, I accepted the position of town-clerk for one year. This was a new experience and I enjoyed it very much. Through this office, I got acquainted with other people, not my members— people who many times had strange ideas on how to run a community. The word "community" was, for some, just a means to become richer instead of a community to be, in general, a better place to live.

The church and parsonage became beautiful places. The parsonage, especially with its surroundings, was an example of what a progressive town should have—a green lawn, a fruit orchard in back and nice shrubbery, always cultivated properly.

Returning one time, many years later, I noticed the town did not show much growth in population and other developments, but the church property was still kept in good condition.

As much as we liked the Merricourt parish and its countryside of stable farmers, we felt we should move to a larger field with a greater potential. The ministers in the state conference were usually well-known to the people, because the conferences brought many people together. Also, during Mission Festivals, an outside speaker was always invited. Thus, when a vacancy took place, the people knew to whom to send a call. To us came such a "call" from a three-church parish in Hebron, North Dakota.

Chapter 16
HEBRON, NORTH DAKOTA

We accepted the "call" from Hebron with great joy, knowing the new field would demand from me what Merricourt could not do. We moved to Hebron in December of 1928.

Hebron lies about sixty miles from Bismarck, west of the Missouri River and about thirty-five miles from Dickinson. Hebron has many old settlers, originally from Germany. Their descendants farmed on a big scale. A fair number were large-scale stock rangers. The largest percentage of the German people were Russia Germans. They, too, succeeded in the Hebron area and were predominantly grain farmers. Hebron lies in a valley and had good transportation by rail and free-way east and west. A brick factory existed in Hebron for many years and put out the finest brick in the west. It employed as many as two hundred men.

The Reich German colony had a large church, parsonage and parish house and boasted of a big membership. There were other churches in Hebron, such as Lutheran, Baptist, Adventist and a number of smaller ones.

The Congregational Church, one English-speaking and the other German-speaking, was smaller in membership. My parish of three churches again demanded much driving, because one church was in Glen Ullen, thirteen miles east and another in the country, sixteen miles out. The parsonage was in Hebron and was owned by all three churches. As in other parishes, the churches were served alternately. For the youth work, all gathered in Hebron on Sunday nights. Glen Ullen and the country church (Bethanien) were smaller in membership compared to Hebron. Economically, this parish was tops, with rich farmers and well-to-do businessmen.

For church-related business matters, the members of all three churches would come together, usually in Hebron. Otherwise, each church conducted its own business matters locally. There was a good, progressive spirit prevailing in the parish and this good-will encouraged me in my church work very much. To prove that there really was a venturesome spirit, we hosted the general conference, which met every two years. Here, it met June 22-26, 1932. To have a large enough meeting place, we pitched a large tent that seated twenty-five hundred people. The city hall was used for the common kitchen. Lodging was provided free, not only by people in the community, but by other churches as well. Many guests stayed with the farmers, who usually had large homes. A very nominal charge was made for lunch and dinner, but breakfast was free.

To have things run smoothly and to expedite the arrangement, we constructed a large office next to the tent across the street from the parsonage. When all the registration of the delegates and non-delegates was complete, including the many outsiders who came on Sunday morning and afternoon, the number came to two thousand. The acting president of Redfield College, Professor Helmuth Schulz, wrote me a letter, stating that this was the largest attended and the best organized general conference ever held. It really was a great success.

The success of this conference gave my parish members just the lift they needed, because many were anxious and had strong misgivings about their ability to host so many people.

The young people in the parish loved to sing. For this big conference, we organized a mass-choir, directed by a member of the English Congregational Church, who was a music and choir teacher in the local high school. Her talent in directing a choir was exceptional, and she performed her task at this conference with the greatest of joy.

The membership of the local church began to grow faster than I had expected. The youth work on Sunday nights was the best in my ministry. They were always willing to come to church and learn. Aside from singing, Bible reading, and discussion, we had Bible-verse contests. People volunteered to memorize Bible verses and then on Sunday night competed with other boys or girls. Those watching would try to match the contestants and then some other Sunday be prepared to stand up and be challenged. I counted the verses one night of one of the competitors and she actually recited 150 verses. Then we had Bible drills, to get better acquainted with the books of the Bible. Sunday night with the

young people was usually the high point of the week.
Another highly important event with lasting results was the winter we had our evangelistic meetings, also in Hebron. Our Russia German people have a pietistic background. Through the years, they would hold these annual prayer meetings, in which the minister would try to bring about a personal commitment to Christ. This commitment was not brought about by just rising or holding up an arm, indicating a decision for Christ. No, it meant going down on your knees and praying until you came to the recognition that your sins were forgiven and that Christ had accepted you. Usually, the congregation would sing a few songs, and the minister would talk about the need of a conversion. After the talk, a gospel song was sung, and then on the knees again for serious prayer. Sometimes, when the Holy Spirit was especially with us, as many as thirty to fifty would pray simultaneously. Some more singing would follow, and again down to prayer. In great awakenings, hundreds of people would be converted. In our case in Hebron, 160 made commitments. What a difference these evangelistic meetings made in the growth of our church! We do not, of course, claim this to be the only way to find one's road to a loving God. God has many ways in which people find Him, but this was the custom with Russia German older people. Today, this custom has been largely given up. Personally, I know and appreciate the blessings those meetings have brought. The many changed people who joined the church, and the time and labor these committed people gave to the church was amazing. A new life! A new creation! How much we could use committed people today!

The last year in Hebron, I was also to serve another church. The local English Congregational Church was without a pastor and hoped I would serve it on Sunday nights before the youth meeting. I accepted the request and tried to do my best. It meant not only additional calling to do, but also to have another Sunday bulletin to mimeograph, one in German and one in English, every week. I kept up this schedule until we left Hebron. I felt this was a church that matched my energy; it was a challenge to me for the whole time that we were there.

Financially, this was also our best field. Our monthly grocery bill never exceeded ten dollars. The farmers would bring us flour, cream, milk, cheese, vegetables, and many other things for the house. For two winters, my wife's parents stayed with us and to keep him occupied, my father-in-law asked me to buy a cow for him to take care of. That plan suited me just right, for in back of the parsonage, we had a good barn with a hay-loft. One of our members, a Mr. Schatz, a very active member in the parish, sold me a cow with a calf at a very low price and I gladly accepted and thanked him profusely. The hay was also cheap and plentiful. And so, the wish of my father-in-law was fulfilled. From this cow, we had all the cream we needed, all the butter we wanted and even cheese.

Our family grew in number. So far, we had Vernon, born in Canada, Grace, born in Washburn, North Dakota, and now in Hebron, North Dakota, on July 25, 1929, came Margie. She was born in the parsonage. Young Dr. Nelson delivered her. Witnessing the birth (the only one of the children), I observed the young doctor and noticed that he was highly nervous, expecting complications, but all proceeded normally.

Looking into the future with three children, not knowing what vicissitudes we might encounter, we thought of going back to school to continue our education. Both of us agreed and, in the late summer, we sold our furniture and such items as we could spare, and moved to Grand Forks, North Dakota, where I hoped to work for my master's degree. It was considered somewhat daring in those days to leave a good parish, sell out, and with three children uproot yourself and start all over among total strangers. We knew, however, what we were doing.

Chapter 17
BACK TO SCHOOL—
UNIVERSITY OF NORTH DAKOTA

With three children in the family, it was out of the question to advertise for an apartment. We needed a furnished house, not too far away from the University and grade schools. We advertised for a house two weeks before moving and in a week an offer of a two-story furnished house came. The owner, knowing who we were, said: "I will rent this house to you much cheaper than I would someone else; you also have the right to sublease the upstairs." We were pleased and paid a month's rent in advance. In a few days, we moved into the house. It was an old house, two stories and a basement. The furniture was average, but we felt one year would do with what there was. The upstairs we rented to a young couple with whom we soon developed a pleasant relationship. He taught at the University.

It was now time to have an interview with the head of the graduate division, Dr. Breitwieser. He was most helpful in lining up my course of study and in choosing the title of the thesis I had to write to obtain the master's degree.

The title of my thesis was, "Type and Nature of German Publications in North Dakota." The "major" in my studies was German literature. With this major, I had to be guided by the head of the German department, Dr. Beck.

I had complete freedom in my program of study. Periodically, I had meetings with Dr. Beck. Other subjects and teachers were: Dr. Breitwieser, philosophy; Dr. Beck, German literature; Dr. Telford, psychology; Dr. Corn, Biblical literature; and Miss Hicks, pottery.

Mrs. Gross also took courses under Dr. Corn in the Wesley College, a Methodist institution across the street from the University campus. The University and Wesley College worked well together for many years.

For the children, too, we were able to have good teachers who took an interest in the whole family. We can truthfully say that our year in Grand Forks was a wonderful experience.

For my thesis, it was necessary for me to make trips to Bismarck, New Salem, Richardson, Ashley, Dickinson, Hebron, Fargo, Denhoff, McClusky and Wishek, to look up issues of the German papers on file there. It was most revealing to find so many German newspapers in those early days in North Dakota. On the other hand, it seems normal that, with so many German people coming into North Dakota from Germany, Russia and other European countries, that they would soon establish a news media to maintain their German identity.

As I studied these many papers and their titles, it became quite obvious that some had strong sympathies with Germany. Other newspapers soon came out in English and later disappeared altogether. Of the many German papers in North Dakota, only two, The *Dakota Freie Presse* and *Der Staats-Anzeiger* maintained a long life, although they were later printed out of state.

The material, gathered and analyzed, made valuable material for my thesis. Finished copies of my master's thesis are found in the North Dakota State Library and in the University of North Dakota, Grand Forks, North Dakota.

In the last few years (1969-1972) much literature has appeared about the Russia German people in the United States—their migrations in history, their accomplishments, and so on. Since nothing had ever before been written about the early German papers, especially in North Dakota, where we find so many German people, my thesis was a source book for many organizations, and even libraries, so much so that it was photographed many times and also translated into German for information, in Stuttgart, Germany.

The thesis was accepted in the University by the graduate department. Later in the year in the University, I was among six others elected into the educational fraternity, Phi Delta Kappa.

When we moved to Grand Forks, we had a little money saved up, and with the money realized through the sale of our furniture, we seemed to have enough to pull us through except for the concern of what could happen when we assumed a new charge again and had to buy furniture to start full-scale housekeeping. As so many times before, somehow, ways and means were always forthcoming.

The state conference superintendent one day wrote me a letter, asking if I would serve two German-speaking churches, Elliot and Englevale, not far from Grand Forks, and within close proximity of one another. I was more than happy for this offer. It was about an hour's drive from Grand Forks. After the service, I was able to come home the same day, even in wintertime. The membership of these churches was small. They were two good little churches, consisting mainly of farmers of good standing in the community. They seemed to be a settlement of relatives, banding together and doing well.

Most of the time, I drove alone to serve these churches. My wife and children would attend the local Congregational Church, with Reverend Allan the minister. In fact, attending this church in Grand Forks, the family became acquainted with the difference in preaching between Reverend Allan and myself. Reverend Allan was not a forceful preacher, but calm and friendly. I, on the other hand, was more forceful and variating in the tone of speaking— sometimes loud, other times soft. And so, one evening, sitting in the front room and talking about church, our eldest daughter made this remark: "Daddy, you are a good father, but you are not a good preacher. In the first place, you shout so loud and then you want to be kind. First, you scare the people and then again you want to love them." I could not help thinking of the Bible reference, "Out of the mouths of Babes, you shall hear the truth." Reverend Allan had been especially nice to our daughter Grace.

Soon another prospect was in the process of development. The German Conference maintained a Mission in Argentina that started there in 1923. Three pastors had been there until now, each under a six-year contract, except one serving five years. The Mission Committee was in search of a suitable man as missionary to Argentina. My wife and I agreed it would be a great experience to go to Argentina as a missionary serving our German people there. The work would be in the German language and the going might sometimes be rough, but we were determined to hand in our name. Finishing school in June of 1934, we waited until August before the commission came through. Feverishly, we made preparation and, by late September, we were on our way to Argentina.

Chapter 18
SIX YEARS IN ARGENTINA AND BRAZIL

The German Congregational Church, a branch of the Congregational Church (now the United Church of Christ) organized and maintained the Mission in Argentina since 1923. It supplied the German-speaking pastors through the years.

When I was chosen to be the missionary to Argentina, a commissioning service in Fredonia, North Dakota, was announced, and to a special evening service, each church in the conference was to send two delegates and the pastor. For an occasion of this sort, the people usually would come in large numbers, from far and near. The church was filled to capacity. After a brief sermon, Mrs. Gross, the children and I were seated on the chancel, facing the congregation. More brief words and well wishes by other pastors followed. Then, the congregation rose and the Gross family knelt for the special prayer of commission. To my great surprise, the Merricourt double quartet sang two of the favorite songs we used to sing when we lived in Merricourt.

All preparations were now made. Passports, health papers, letters of recommendation were secured and, with a brief stop in Chicago, our destination was New York and from there with the steamer *Southern Cross,* to Argentina, arriving October 3, 1934. Reverend George Kuhn welcomed us and finally took us to his home in Viale, Entre Rios. The Kuhns had three children, losing one in infancy.

Our trip to Argentina on the sea was rather interesting. The list of passengers included people from all walks of life, business people in large numbers, many vacationing, others traveling for health reasons. An unusually large number on this ship were priests, cardinals and other Catholic members on the way to Argentina for the Eucharistic Congress that was hosted by the Argentina Catholic Church.

The ship's officials usually have elaborate programs aboard ship to keep the passengers occupied and happy. Every day a new program was posted on the bulletin board. Also, athletic contests were part of the transit's program. As a rule, in case of a Sunday on board ship, a service was arranged. At one such Sunday service, I was the speaker. The service was rather well attended. Outside of the service at which I officiated, there was also early Mass arranged for the large Catholic contingent on the ship.

A special ceremony was arranged when we crossed the equator, consisting of music, speeches and dunking. Some special guests were selected and a brief write-up given, pointing out, in our case, the courage of a family with children going to an unknown land of totally different customs, language and people.

What made the whole character of this passenger group so different was the many Catholic clergymen on board—eighty of them—and all going to Argentina. It was a daily ritual for most of them to pray their rosary, or walk up and down the deck of the ship, alone, or sometimes a woman with a priest, reciting the rosary. In the mornings, these faithful Catholics were on their knees and going through their prayer ritual.

What startled me above everything else was the excessive drinking and gambling on board ship by the Catholics. I went into the barroom just to see what was going on after I was told by others about this sight in the bar. I saw it and, what I saw, I did not like. In one case, the clergyman gambling had his clergy collar open to signify, so I was told, that he was not gambling as an official Catholic clergyman. The other thing that surprised me about these delegates to the Eucharistic Congress was the capacity of alcohol they were able to consume.

One of the orderlies on board, responsible for the cleanliness in the various rooms, looked very disgusted to me one morning. I asked him, "What is the matter, why such a long face?"

He looked at me and said: "These——priests, in the evening, you can't get them out of the barroom and in the morning you can't get them off their knees to clean up the place." I could not argue with the orderly, for what I saw substantiated what he said. This was a new experience for me to see these representatives acting in a group.

With so many Catholics getting off in Buenos Aires, Argentina, our going through customs was much easier too. The captain of the ship stood at the gangplank as we got off and, when it came to me, he said to the official: "Another church official." Not that I expected any customs difficulties—I had all the necessary papers and documents to enter Argentina—but just seeing how easy it is for some people to enter a country surprised me.

It was not since I had left Russia that I again saw the horse-carriages, drawn either by one or two horses. Reverend Kuhn and a member of his church met us as we got off the ship, and took us to a hotel. This was a new experience here too—language, food, and rooms, all different. Reverend Kuhn, having been here for more than six years, was of great help to us, speaking the language and knowing his way around. The next day, we took the train to the province of Entre Rios, where most of our churches were located at that time.

There were many adjustments to make and customs to get used to. The seasons here are reversed, which meant going from a cold climate in a few days into a hot climate. The other experience was the lack of modern conveniences.

Possibly the greatest difference between Argentina and the United States was the slow rate of speed at which the people in Argentina worked, and the many people required to do a job that, in the States, was done by half the personnel. The roads were poor, not kept up, without warning signs at dangerous spots. In rains, driving was practically an impossibility. The province of Entre Rios, where most of our churches were, had a wonderful dark soil, suited for flax, grain, corn, castor beans, and vegetables.

How did our people get here? Where did they come from, and what brought them here?

Most of them came from Russia, where some lived near the Volga and others near Odessa, the two regions that received the Germans during the reign of Catherine II in 1763 and the reign of Alexander I in 1804. They left Russia after their promised rights were abrogated, some leaving for North America and some to South America.

It was during the presidency of Dr. Avellaneda (1874-80) that an intensive colonization program began. During his time in office, he was instrumental in bringing 268,500 farmers into Argentina and Brazil, having sent men earlier to become familiar with the type of land available. In 1873-76, German explorers had visited both North America and South America to report back their findings.

There was intensive rivalry between Brazil and Argentina. Each country wanted Russia German farmers as soon as possible. On the trip to South America, agents on the ship would warn the people that Argentina's soil was not suited for growing wheat. The result, however, was that most of the farmers came to Argentina, settling in Diamante, Entre Rios, in January of 1878.

After spending four weeks in Diamante, the colonists were brought out into the country, and after eighteen weeks more of waiting and planning, a number of villages were established. The government was really against establishing villages and wanted to have the colonists scattered individually in many places. The colonists, however, won out. Thus, the following villages were established: Marienthal (Valle Maria), Marienfeld (Spathenkutter), Koehler (Salta), Pfeifer (San Francisco), and Aldea Protestante in October 1878. All of these villages are still existing today and are in the Department Diamante.

Aldea San Antonio is the cradle of our German work in Argentina. Other areas where we have some churches are: Almada, Aranguren, Basavilvaso, Bovril, Crespo, Buena Vista, Viole, Camp, and a number of others.

When the call came to organize a church, the German Conference sent Reverend J. Hoeltzer, a Volga German pastor, to Urdinarrain, Entre Rios (Aldea San Antonio lies out in the country, away from the railroad). Many of his countrymen greeted him with joy and expectancy. Reverend Hoeltzer was an able organizer and at home in dealing with his people. Within days, meetings were called for the purpose of organizing a Congregational Church. At first, Reverend Hoeltzer explained the fundamental beliefs and practices of our church, then gave the people the opportunity to ask questions.

It must be indicated here why the people wanted a Congregational Church. German people from the Reich had come to Argentina, long before the Russia German settlers did. That was true throughout South America. It was normal to think that the German State Church would be concerned about its people in the Diaspora. The German State Church in Argentina is called "The La Plata Synode" and in Brazil "The Rio Grandenser Synode." The Missouri Lutheran Church was also very active in Argentina, and so were the Seventh Day Adventists who, by the way, did a tremendous piece of work with their hospitals and schools.

The La Plata Synode had many churches wherever Germans had settled, so that it was natural for the Russia Germans to join. The financial contributions amounted to very little. In fact, the appeal to join their church was made repeatedly in their paper, because it cost nothing to do so. The *Deutscher Volksbund* was a widely distributed German paper whose purpose was to unite all the German-speaking people in foreign countries, to help them build German schools, maintain German libraries, and advance the German cause throughout South America. An *Jahrbuch* (yearbook) appears and is distributed far and wide. (What I am describing here is largely taken from the 1937 Jahrbuch.)

The Missouri Lutheran Church also was in Argentina and Brazil before we came upon the scene.

Why then was it necessary for us to come to Argentina and to Brazil? What was motivating so many Russia German people to want to join a different church?

Through the years in Russia, and also to a degree, far back in Germany, our Russia German people were not only loyal churchgoers, but also firm believers in prayer meetings. On the Volga and especially around Odessa in most colonies, our people had their prayer meetings in the homes or in some larger community building. The La Plata Synode frowned upon this "church within the church," and took a stern stand against the prayer meetings in all of their parishes. This attitude on the part of the pastors of the church and, above all, the ridiculing of the prayer meetings, was too much for our people.

This type of attitude against the prayer meetings was also propagated by the Missouri Lutheran Church.

Another reason why so many Russia German people joined our denomination was the church-freedom within our church. The church members had something to say. And, as far as the prayer meetings were concerned, our ministers even encouraged and, in many cases, sponsored them and participated in all the prayer meetings. Sunday school, worship, prayer meetings, and youth work were, for us, the fundamental activities of pastor and people.

Possibly the strongest factor causing the Russia German people to come over to the Congregational Church was the entanglement of the Reich German La Plata Synode in Argentina, in worldly things and in Reich German politics. During the war in the thirties, the Reich German churches even had the Hitler Hakenkreuz in their churches, and many gave the Hitler salute as they greeted each other. Our people had little sympathy, if any, with such a political entanglement, and were patient for many years. But now there seemed to be a way out.

As indicated earlier, the cradle of our denomination in Argentina is in Aldea Protestante, Urdinarrain, Entre Rios. This village was settled in October 1878 and is, to this day, a flourishing village with a big church and schoolhouse. Now, it is ninety-five per cent Congregational.

The La Plata Synode did not remain inactive, seeing so many of its members leaving their church. They would ridicule our church, saying it really is not a church; it is not a German church and their pastors are not well-educated pastors, and so on, but, all this notwithstanding, the people came to join our denomination.

When I assumed my responsibilities, we made our home in Urdinarrain, a city of about five thousand people. It was a railroad city, with a mixture of people, German and Argentine.

The local church was, next to Aldea Protestante, the largest in membership. The church was of a soft brick, high ceilinged, with a high window and brick floor. The house we rented was near the church. It had three bedrooms, front room and a large kitchen and patio, with adjoining orchard.

To get acquainted with the mission field, my colleague and I proceeded to visit all of the churches of our mission in the following provinces: Entre Rios, Formosa, Chaco, Misiones, and Buenos Aires. In the meantime, with the family settled, we had our choice to send our children either to the national or provincial elementary school. We chose the provincial school. Children learn fast. In three months, our children got along with the everyday Spanish. For Mrs. Gross and myself, it took much longer. Our children would say, "Mother knows more, but Daddy talks more Spanish."

The main transportation in Argentina was by rail. To travel by car was very risky because of the poor roads and, in case of mechanical trouble, a garage would be hard to find. To go by train, one had to have the right change when purchasing a ticket, especially early in the morning. On short distances, we usually went second class. Long distance, and overnight in the trains, we went first class. Argentina had three railway systems: the English, the French and their own, the Nacional. The French railway was of a narrow gauge track. Aside from the train, Entre Rios and *coche motores* for short distances. They were very practical and the service was good.

To best and most quickly see most of our churches, Reverend Kuhn and I went by first-class rail to the main church in each area of our churches, hoping the neighboring church members would attend where we stopped. The members responded well and the round trip was completed in two months. It was a trip not only encouraging for the future of our work, promising in every respect, but also a rare experience to behold the many sights of rare beauty, especially in Misiones.

When we returned from our lengthy trip, Mr. Kuhn and I sat down to assign each other the churches to be served by each. He lived in Viale, the opposite side of the province from my side, thus, both of us were able to serve our churches with less time spent on the road. We had, at the time, twenty-two churches to serve by five pastors. Only one church had a pastor every Sunday, and one church had services once a month. Other churches were served twice and four times a year. In the meantime, they had services led by one of the members, either reading a sermon or giving a devotional talk. In spite of the shortage of pastors, the mission field grew. New invitations to come and organize churches came every few months.

Our members in Entre Rios and in Formosa and most of those in the Argentine Chaco, were Volga Russia Germans. A few in the Chaco were Russia German from Odessa, and all those in Misiones were from Wolhynien, who came from the United States, Brazil and from Poland.

When we arrived in Argentina, there were, in reality, only four pastors serving churches in Entre Rios, Chaco and Misiones. With the fast growth of our church, especially in the territory of Misiones, more pastors had to be found. In Misiones, we found a well-educated young man who was a teacher, Ludwig Serfas, who, after taking some training in the Methodist Seminary in Buenos Aires, was ordained into the ministry. He moved from Buenos Aires to Entre Rios and there served a parish of six churches. Reverend G. Geier, also a former teacher who was later ordained, served seven churches. Reverend Kuhn, who had been in Argentina six years when we arrived, served eleven churches. When we arrived, and shortly thereafter, it was necessary for me to serve most of the distantly located churches, because many new ones were in need of more information of the nature of our church and needed guidance in becoming organized into a Congregational church. The work-load became very high, in fact, unbearable. In addition to carrying administrative responsibility, traveling thousands of kilometers every month, doing the corresponding with pastors, with churches, and answering the new requests from Brazil for admission into our denomination, as well as serving fourteen churches, the cry for more pastoral assistance became louder and louder. But, this was not all. From every direction, voices were heard, "We should have a religious paper to get information from one another and to serve as a fellowship medium." Within a few months, a paper, *Der Herold* was established and issued twice a month. I was requested to assume the editorial writing and get all the material ready to be printed by a firm in Buenos Aires. Many times, I wrote my editorials while riding on the train. This church paper was a godsend for our work. The paper was liked, because it was a religious paper and the people could participate in its content. Later, when the work expanded in Brazil, *Der Herold* was sent there too. It truly became a paper anxiously anticipated every two weeks. This church paper is to this day, serving our churches in Argentina and Brazil better than we had ever anticipated.

Traveling in Argentina was often fraught with danger, discomfort and strange circumstances. The traveler in Argentina usually travels with a weapon—a revolver, dagger, or both. Many times, my members would advise me to carry a weapon. My answer was always, "I would not have a chance." My really great surprise was one afternoon in Misiones, before going home, when I had to stay overnight in a hotel. I asked for a single room for one night. The proprietor asked, "Where do you come from?"

I said, "From North America."

He said, "I thought so, but we have no rooms for one person only." When I went to occupy my room, the second bed was already occupied by a man with a dagger on the table and a revolver under his pillow. I took a deep breath and, with a silent prayer in my heart, I went to bed.

The discomforts were largely in connection with transportation after leaving the train. To get to your destination, a bus, camion (truck), or wagon was available. With the bad roads, breakdowns of vehicles, or heavy rains, many delays upset your program. Then, there were the many insects, bugs and lack of sanitary conditions, which affected your life very much.

To defend myself against these pests, I always carried with me some eucalyptus oil and quinine pills. In mosquito-infested places, the hotels would provide a netting over your bed to keep out the mosquitoes. Since, in most cases, these suspended nettings had big enough holes in them for a mouse to come to visit you, I would always carry with me needle and thread. The water in hotels and other public places, including restaurants, was not drinkable. Having been a teetotaler for many years, I started to drink, both wine and beer. Carbonated water also was available. At one place in Formosa, the temptation to drink water, not tea, got the best of me. On my way home, my church member brought me to the country store where I could take the bus the next morning. I stayed the night, sleeping on a cot in an open enclosure. I was so thirsty for water that I yielded to the temptation to drink from a barrel standing nearby. My thirst quenched, I went to bed and off to sleep. At night, I was awakened by a rider who came to the same place to stay the night. He dismounted, unsaddled his horse, and then led him to the same barrel to quench the animal's thirst.

In the Chaco, too, where cotton was grown, we had a number of churches. My stay was with one of the members who had a well dug by hand, about six feet wide and about fifteen feet deep. The water was drawn with tee-post structures and pail at the end. All the water they used came from this well. One day, I was tempted to go to the well to draw fresh water. What I saw was not totally unfamiliar to me, because I had seen it in Russia, again and again, where they had community wells. I was in for a surprise, however. From above, I could see living creatures in the well: insects, frogs, and creatures whose names I did not know. Was this the water the people used in their homes? Yes, for cooking and to drink. Knowing this, I drew a bucket of water. There were so many living creatures in that pail of water that I thought I was eating soup. I reached for my handkerchief, held it over the pail and drank to quench my thirst. Well, I am still alive!

What topped it all off was the experience on another trip in Formosa when we traveled by camion (truck). These camions would haul groceries to outlying grocery stores. On such a camion, I was traveling to reach my church. On the way, we came to a low place and our truck got stuck in the mud. There were three of us traveling with the driver and his companion. While they were extracting the truck out of the mud, the three of us looked for water. A short distance away was a farmer. We went there to ask for water. He had a large barrel lying on a wagon outside. He took us to where the barrel was, and one of my companions reached for the stopper to pull it when the farmer said, "Hold it, let me do it." What was the situation here? It turned out, so the farmer told us, that he kept a snake in the barrel to keep the water cool. Did we drink of the water? Yes, all three of us. If it did not kill the farmer, it would not kill us, we reasoned.

Having an adventurous nature, I did not mind these inconveniences too much. In time, one got used to this type of frontier life. There was a certain thrill to it, and I certainly got my share of it every time I traveled north and later also on the way to Brazil.

Whenever a pastor came to a field, there were, without exception, some other pastoral functions to carry out, such as baptisms, confirmations or weddings. In the six years I served our churches in Argentina, I baptized over six hundred children and adults. There was not a single morning worship without baptisms at the end of the service. With the large families of our people and the infrequent appearance of the pastor, there were as many as sixteen baptisms to perform at one service alone.

In Formosa, I had the strangest baptismal service. Our services were all conducted in the German language. The listeners were not always German people. There had already been a good many intermarriages and, in case of one spouse being a Russia German, children had to be baptized. In this particular service, the people present at the out-of-door service were a mixed group: German, Argentine, Spanish and even one Britisher. Nine children, from a few-months old baby to a 19-year-old young man, awaited baptism. In back of the improvised church, several men were talking and smoking while I preached. I suppose they did not understand what I was talking about anyway. The baptismal candidates were all in front of me waiting to be baptized. They were arranged according to age and with them their parents and, in most cases, also their sponsors. When I came with the baptismal chalice to the two-year-old, he eyed me suspiciously and, just as I sprinkled water on his forehead, he hit me right on my forehead. This produced considerable laughter, especially in the back of the room. The mother of the child was embarrassed to no end, however, and later apologized.

To show how much our Russia Germans adhered to childhood teaching and to tradition, I was asked to officiate at a marriage in a small town in the Chaco. An Argentine of a high position was being married to one of our German girls who worked in the city. In Argentina, the civil marriage takes precedence. Our German people, however, always had the church wedding immediately following the civil ceremony. This couple, coming to my hotel room to be married, had a civil marriage performed, but the wife, a German girl, insisted that I perform the marriage ceremony and so I did. They were very happy and thanked me profusely, also giving me an honorarium of no mean amount.

There was a distinct difference in the customs and practices between the Russia Germans in Entre Rios and those living in Misiones.

The Misiones people (Wolhynier), throughout their lives, had prayer meetings wherever they lived. They all knew how to pray. In Misiones, they were without a pastor for many years, coming together, however, regularly every Sunday. Upon entering the church, they first knelt down to pray and then occupied a pew. After they joined our denomination, they kept up this practice and I loved to see them do so. In Entre Rios, the service was more formal. The prayer meetings were always a blessing to me. Laymen would often help to lead the prayer meetings. In Entre Rios, especially in the Urdinarrain church, the prayer meeting was usually well attended and of exceptionally deep religious nature. The hymn books were very few, so the leader would announce the hymn, phrase by phrase, and the rest would pick up the words of the hymn. In fact, it was seldom necessary to have any books. The leader would simply start a gospel song and the rest followed. There was something moving in this unstructured type of prayer meeting. They were deeply inspiring. Many times since have I yearned for the spiritual experiences of those years in Argentina. Many times, I felt sorry for my family, that they had to be alone so much of the time. The three youngsters especially at these years needed their father with them more. Because I was away most of the time, we felt the family could just as well live in Buenos Aires. This would give the children a better education in the Methodist American grammar and high schools and they would have the fellowship of American young people and especially keep up the English language. This was decided upon, and the family moved to the big city. Mrs. Gross was asked to be in charge of the girls in the dormitory, thus giving her the opportunity to be with the children all of the time. Later, Mrs. Gross also did some substitute teaching in the same grammar school. We were pleased with the American grammar and high school. It also had a college in Argentina, Ramos Mejia, where the courses were taught in Spanish. Combined, the two schools were called Ward College.

During our time, the schools had the following administrators: Dr. Fred Aden, director; Dr. S. P. Maddock, vice-director and Reverend S. S. McWilliams, treasurer.

Ward College was founded in November of 1913 in memory of Mrs. Nancy Gracey Ward of Sewickly, Pennsylvania, at the instigation of, and through a gift from, her son, Mr. George B. Ward, at the time head of the Ward Baking Company.

Ward College was founded by the Board of Foreign Missions of the Methodist Church. It is noteworthy to remark that the Methodist Church had received official permission from the Argentine government, as recorded in the archives of the nation, to work in Argentina as early as 1835.

Ward College had a very good reputation in Argentina. Children from many countries attended this school, even children of Argentine official families. During our time, the son of the city mayor attended Colegio Ward. Mrs. Gross and our children were the beneficiaries of a much needed fellowship in a foreign country and, in addition, the three children received the best possible education one could expect outside of the United States.

The Methodist Church also had a highly rated seminary in Buenos Aires, headed by Dr. Stockwell. The Disciples of Christ and our Argentine Mission cooperated with this seminary. It was our pleasure in subsequent years also to become acquainted with a number of the Methodist pastors in the inland and in Brazil.

As our German work progressed, so too increased the propaganda against us on the part of the La Plata Synod and the Reich Germans. Those were the Hitler years in Argentina, as well as throughout the South American countries, wherever the Reich Germans were found. The locally read papers, the *Der Russlanddeutsche, Die La Plata Zeitung,* and *Der Volkbund der Deutschen Im Aussland,* all were Hitleristic and loyal to Germany. In the face of all of this Hitler propaganda, I took issue in my editorials in our paper, *Der Herold,* pleading with our people not to be swept away by political activity in our churches and not to bite the hand that was feeding them, namely Argentina. It had some effect, but in view of the constant and daily propaganda, some of our Congregational members turned to Hitler for rescue. To show how deeply involved the Hitler regime became in Argentina, let me refer to one case in particular.

In my travels to visit my churches, I was always on the alert to read English and German names. Finding or reading such names, I acquainted myself and, thus, made good contacts. One time, coming to my church in the Chaco, one of my members informed me that a certain Mr. Pfohl, from the town of Barrangeros, was there, showing slides of Germany and highly praising what Hitler was now doing in Germany, collecting money at the same time. I thought that this was incredible and decided to look into this on my way home. Stopping off in Barrangeros, I looked up the Anderson Clayton Cotton Gin factory, the name of which I had spotted on a former trip.

Coming into the yard, I inquired about the jefe (the chief) and was led into his office. He introduced himself as Mr. Pfohl, the man who earlier had shown Hitler slides to my people. On checking further, I found that he was also the German vice-counsel for that region.

Later, when calling on my family in Buenos Aires, I reported this to the head office of the Clayton company, only to be told that it could not be; the man was too busy to do any sort of outside work. I did not get anywhere with the company. I then took it up with the American Legion in Buenos Aires, of which I was a member. It did not take very long and the Hitlerist, Mr. Pfohl, was dismissed.

The high point in the Hitler propaganda came in 1935-37 when two clippings in *Der Stuermer* were sent to me. *Der Stuermer* was the main propaganda paper of the Hitler party in South America. A copy of this paper was never sent to me, but most of my people received it and then, of course, I would become informed about it. To my great surprise, one Sunday this degrading sheet was personally distributed to my people in the town of Basavilbaso, as the people came out of church. This was done deliberately, no doubt because of the stand I took in our church paper, *Der Herold*. What I read in this issue of *Der Stuermer* reads, interpreted, like this:

"Be careful what you read in *Der Herold*, the church paper of the Congregationalists. It is written by a certain F. W. Gross, a missionary in Argentina. Don't believe him, he is a communist and a Jew, and to eat off Jewish tables, is good eating."

A clipping was also sent to me by one of our pastors in Brazil, who also was receiving the *Der Stuermer*. In this clipping, my name was not mentioned, but we could clearly tell that it was I who was referred to. The Hitler propaganda was so extensive that whenever an Argentine met a German, he took it for granted that he was Hitlerite. The Hitler propaganda was carried on through papers, magazines, slides, secret meetings, and speeches in frontier places, like with my people in distant areas. Anyone taking up any sort of action against Hitlerism was branded a "Communist" and a "Jew," as it was in my case. The same pattern of Hitler propaganda was carried on in Brazil too. What puzzled me no end was that neither government did anything to counteract this vicious propaganda.

At the end of the school year, in 1939, my family and I moved to Concordia, Entre Rios, a city farther north, thus closer to the churches I was serving. Concordia was a port city with many more means of transportation than Urdinarrain. Concordia also had a hospital, clinic, good schools, and a good residential section. We were able to get a good three-bedroom house in a desirable section of town. There was also a doctor on our block who understood some English.

We came to Argentina with three children, a son, Vernon, and two daughters, Grace and Margie. Now, there was evidence that the family would increase. We felt relieved that we were now in a city with all the needed medical help, should a need arise. Arrangements were made for Mrs. Gross to enter the local hospital maintained by the government through lotteries. When the time for delivery came, Mrs. Gross developed periodic labor pains and called the nurse (sister) to notify the doctor. The nurse, however, declined to call the doctor, saying, "You are not due yet, you have not had any children the last nine years, it will take more time for you to deliver." Mrs. Gross knew better; the child was coming, and coming in a hurry. She tried to go to the bathroom, but got only as far as behind the door, where the child was born, as she was standing up. She placed it on a newspaper on the mosaic floor. Her roommate called the nurse at once, and this time the nurse came running full speed, apologizing profusely. The child was normal and the arrival on a hard floor did not seem to faze her at all. Nancy May was born March 5, 1939 in Concordia, Entre Rios, Argentina. All children born in Argentina had to be registered with the local office of registration. This I did the following day. The gentleman behind the desk asked me for all the information the questionnaire called for. When I gave him the name, Nancy May, he mused and said, "May, yes, Nancy, no." The point was that Argentina did not accept names that did not have an equivalent in Spanish; hence, he would not accept "Nancie." I told him, for us she is Nancy May and that he could put down whatever he wanted. He then registered her as Anna May Gross. We had been told that there were many cases of people having difficulty in the right of choosing their own names for their children. Some cases even resorted to the courts.

    The northernmost territory (later called province) of our church work was Misiones, that had a very fertile, red soil. The people bought their forest land, chopped down the trees and cleared the shrubs and let nature dry the growth. Then the farmers burned the dry foliage, leaving the heavy trees. They planted tobacco seedlings, issued them by the nearby tobacco company (in Bonpland). As I remember, the two kinds of tobaccos were Maryland and Kentucky. Aside from tobacco, this land grew wonderful citrus fruit, pineapple, and all sorts of vegetables, including mandioka.

With the abundance of lumber on hand and the variety of wood, the farmers built their own homes out of the finest of woods. I found a number of houses, with walls and floors of genuine cedar. To enter such a house was a real treat, for the aroma was something to experience.

The roads in the country were rough and rocky. Driving on these in wagons without springs was a punishment unless one knew just how to sit so that your body would act as springs and, thus, absorb the jolting every step of the way. Coming to one's destination from a lengthy trip, whatever apparel one had on would be red. Everything was red, including the money.

BRAZIL

To report about our growing missionary work in Brazil, I must begin with what preceded in Argentina, in the territory of Misiones.

After the world war, many German people from Poland (Wolhynien), Germany, Russia and others, came to take up land in Misiones. Among those from Wolhynien (in Poland), were also German schoolteachers, also taking up land. These teachers were able men and were an asset in the colonies.

Two of these teachers, Mariano Gorski and Henrick Schroeder, were instrumental in bringing our Congregational work into Brazil. After our work was established, through the influence of Mr. Gorski, I called on my predecessor, Reverend C. Kuhn, to visit them in Misiones. On a second visit, in which I accompanied Mr. Kuhn, three churches in Misiones were admitted into our denomination in November of 1934.

These people in Misiones were also, like in Entre Rios, members of the La Plata Synode, but because of their desire to hold prayer meetings, were not tolerated and, in a few cases, simply asked to leave the church. Thus, for a number of years, they independently carried on their church work by themselves, even giving each other the sacrament of communion. They felt the need to become a part of some established church denomination.

We ordained Mr. Mariano Gorski to become the minister of this new field in Misiones. (Mr. Gorski was a Reich German, married in

Poland to a Jewish wife.) Misiones is just a short distance from Brazil and the traffic between the two countries was rather heavy. Soon, it became known that there were also many Wolhynier in Rio Grande do Sul, Brazil. Word came to Reverend Gorski that the state of Rio Grande do Sul had thousands of Wolhynier, most of whom were earlier with the Reich Church, in Brazil called "The Rio Grandeser Synode." This was happy news for Mr. Gorski and, in 1935, resulted in our accepting three churches into our denomination, and a year later, he moved to Brazil, settling in the Guarani area. In his place, a young man of exceptional talent, Mr. Ludwig Serfas, began to serve the churches in Misiones. Later, Mr. Serfas studied in the Methodist Seminary in Buenos Aires, and after his ordination, took a church in Entre Rios. Misiones was then served by me for the rest of the term that I was in Argentina.

Before reporting on the special event of the extension of our work in Brazil, a word of the immigration of the Russia Germans into Brazil must be here recorded.

It was in 1872 that agents went to the United States and to Brazil to find land suitable for agriculture. Reporting very favorably on the land in both countries, emigration took on momentum. A few families went to the United States. In 1875, three hundred families of Volga Germans arrived in Canada and smaller groups came to Brazil. In 1873-74, three thousand Russia Germans arrived in Porto Alegre. These three thousand had to go through many hardships, hunger and misfortune, clashing with the police, and many were killed. In the search for wheatland, they wandered inland; some stayed, but the majority finally reached the state of Parani where they, at last, found soil that grew wheat. To this day, large colonies (many Catholic) of Russia Germans are found in the states of Parani and Santa Catharina. Subsequent groups, especially the Wolhynier, are found further inland in Rio Grande do Sul. South Russia emigrants in larger number are found in the Pampa in southern Argentina, where they found fertile land for growing wheat and other grain. In my six years in Argentina, both North Russian and South Russian Germans were found in the Chaco, and a few scattered in Formosa.

There was strong competition between Argentina and Brazil for immigrants from Russia, each country praising its soil for agriculture. Each of the mentioned countries would make very attractive offers to win immigrants. In the years of 1877 and 1879, thousands left Russia for both Argentina and Brazil. A goodly number that had settled in Porto Alegre or Rio Grande do Sul pulled up stakes and came to Argentina, staying in Entre Rios, the real grain country.

The strongest groups of Russia Germans were from Poland, called the Wolhynier, who settled in Rio Grande do Sul. Before the coming of the Wolhynier, Rio Grande do Sul had many Reich Germans, most of them third-generation Germans.

Among these Wolhynier and Brazil-Reich-Germans, our mission took a foothold.

What was their religious life like? Having practiced the prayer meetings from generation to generation, they hoped to continue the same way in Brazil. While at the same time belonging to an established church, they united with the German Reich Church in Brazil, the "Rio Grandenser Synode." Some had joined the Missouri Lutheran Church. But, they did not feel at home in either of these churches. Both simply did not tolerate them, as they were considered "a church within the church." The Wolhynier tried everything possible to work with the church, but with permission to continue their prayer meeting. But, it was a choice, either quit prayer meetings or leave the church. They left.

The Nature of the Reich-German Church
Before We Began Our Congregational Mission in Brazil.

The source of information is taken from "A Short History of the German Immigration onto Rio Grande do Sul," issued by a commission in 1935, Sao Leopoldo, Rio Grande do Sul.

This source booklet speaks of the first Germans coming into Brazil in 1824 from Germany and settling in Rio Grande do Sul. On this first transport, there were 43 persons. On November 26, 1824 came 81 persons. Of these 124 immigrants, only 18 had any knowledge of the soil, the others representing all kinds of occupations. These first settlers came from the poorhouses, the jails, and many, therefore, were convicts. They were sent to Brazil with good advice and with a Bible, in the hopes that Brazil would be the land to bring them again into good standing in society. Later years, however, indicated the contrary to be the case. President Pinheira spoke of them as "os mais immorais," (much immoral) and hesitated at first to have them settle in Rio Grande do Sul, but finally yielded.

In subsequent years, new settlers came from Germany, so that by 1830, a total of 4,856 persons had come to Rio Grande do Sul. In 1830, Brazil discontinued subsidizing immigrants, feeling it meant neglecting their own people. Rumors of dissatisfaction of their own citizens became stronger and stronger. In 1844, however, new groups from Germany came. In 1844, 66 persons, in 1845, 87 persons and in 1846, 1,515 persons came. In ten years, from 1844 to 1854, in all 4,317 persons settled in Rio Grande do Sul.

In these early years of the Germans in Brazil, there was little, if any, help coming from the churches. The church did not keep pace with the immigration of its people. There were three pastors who seemed to serve the people during these early times: Reverend Ehler, Reverend Voger and Reverend Kligerhoefer. As a result of this scarcity of ministers, the people would find their own pastor who would serve them and, in some cases, also teach their schoolchildren. These new-found ministers very often had strange backgrounds. At one place, the pastor was an alcoholic and a gambler. In another place, the pastor was a military deserter, a noncommissioned officer from Prussia, also an alcoholic. In a third location, the pastor was a barroom owner who had gone through bankruptcy in Porto Alegre. In a fourth place, the minister was a tailor and a surveyor. A fifth pastor had a business on the side and announced from the pulpit that there would be a dance at his place in the afternoon. It was even worse with the Catholics.

What held these spiritually starved people together? There was no influx of pastors from their fatherland and no reliable men as pastors available locally. They had something familiar to them from their childhood: Sunday devotional, the catechism, morning and evening devotionals, table blessings, and reading of the gospels on Sundays. These childhood practices rescued them and saved the church, both Protestant and Catholic.

It was not until 1886 when finally the Rio Grandenser Synode was organized; in other words, sixty-two years after the first

Germans landed in Brazil.

The Missouri Synode began its missionary work in Rio Grande do Sul in 1900. By 1934, it had 26,482 members. Later also came the Baptists and other free churches.

The two strongest churches were, of course, the Rio Grande Synode and Missouri Synode, but neither of these two denominations tolerated what the majority of the people and later also the Wolhynier were accustomed to in the home countries; that is, the prayer meetings.

In time, they heard of our denomination and of the fact that we cooperated and even sponsored prayer meetings. This, for them, was a godsend. From now on, they sought to become part of us.

In a few years, dozens of churches became independent, leading their own services, and hiring a schoolteacher to teach their children. These independent churches, by now, consisted not only of Wolhynier, but also of Reich Germans who had been in Brazil for generations. In time, some of these churches were able to find undenominational pastors who were at least willing to cooperate with these independent churches. The fact that they were without an affiliation with an established church gradually seemed to dawn upon them, and they began to look around for an established church.

These many independent churches searched for a denomination in which there was freedom to worship according to their beliefs and whenever and wherever in the church they could be at the same time a full-fledged member. The answer to their prayer now was coming true.

A "Macedonian Call" came, first through a letter to Reverend Gorski, then through two delegates calling on him to contact me in Argentina for the purpose of getting better acquainted with the Congregational Church. Before I decided to go to Brazil, I suggested that Reverend Gorski, who was in Brazil at the time, and Mr. H. Schroeder take the trip to find out just how many people or members in these independent churches were to be found. These two former schoolteachers made the trip, spent about a week with these people and found them, after hearing about our denomination, ready to join us. They set a tentative date to hold a gathering and hoped that I would be there, and when they were ready to join us, take them up formally. The date of this historical conference was set for January 6-9, 1938, in Paraiso, Cochoeira, Rio Grande do Sul. Reverend M. Gorski and I arrived January 6, and were hosted in the home of one member of the local church. Already, most of the official delegates, including their pastor, had arrived. This conference was first to be their last official meeting and, at the same time, the conference to officially unite with us. These independent churches had only recently adopted the name "Die Evangelische Lutherische Bekenntnis Kirche" (The Evangelical Lutheran Confessional Church), only to give it up for our name. There were meetings every day of the four-day conference from eight o'clock in the morning until late at night, two services on Sunday forenoon, another in the afternoon, and a closing service in the evening. On Sunday morning, two ordinations took place and on Sunday afternoon, the big event of the independent churches and their minister joining our church.

It was the event of my life on Sunday afternoon, January 9, 1938, to see fifty churches with eleven hundred families, making a total of four thousand eight hundred members, affiliating with the Congregational Church. The names of the pastors who joined are as follows: Karl Spittler, Erwin Reich, Heinrich Hirtzel, F. W. Stahlschuss (licentiate), Richard Strauss, Bernhardt Kramer, Albert Glockner and Daniel Ammueller—eight in all. In addition, the transfer to us included a number of church buildings and parsonages. The majority of these churches are financially self-supporting.

This process of uniting with the Congregational Church required not only endless correspondence, but genuine compassion with a people who were disenfranchised from the very essence of Christian life. These people were hungry for the Word of God, and looked up to the existing church for spiritual leadership, but did not get it. Instead, they were hounded and literally alienated from the church. Then, we came upon the scene, not only preaching the kind of message we did, but also sitting down with them, discussing the Word of God and, especially, what they had never seen in their lives before, kneeling down to pray with them. No wonder, as one exclaimed, "Now, we live again!"

The missionary work that was carried on by the Rio Grandenser Synode consisted merely of preaching on Sunday mornings and seeing to it that the children were baptized, confirmed and eventually married. No young people's work and no prayer meetings. For a full-rounded church program, these poor people needed three men: one to preach, another to direct the youth work and a third one to take care of the prayer life of the people. When they found out that in our denomination, the pastor is in charge of all three activities, you could not hold them back from uniting with us.

With the news of this history-making event of thousands joining our church, the anti-propaganda began in full swing. "What? German people joining a non-German church and, in addition, a church represented by a man who is against Hitler? He must be a Jew." But all propaganda, in word and print, did not discourage our people. They now had what their hearts had yearned for for many years. In subsequent years, we placed a man from the States to live in Ijui, Rio Grande do Sul, and we established a school where youngsters could obtain a higher education, largely working themselves through school.

When I left in 1940, we had a mission in Brazil consisting of eight pastors, forty-four churches and five thousand members. The potential for us in Brazil was limitless. The people loved the church and, on Sundays, young and old were in the church.

Chapter 19
RETURN TO THE STATES—LODI, CALIFORNIA

Mrs. Gross was with me on this history-making trip to Misiones and Brazil. On the many travels to distant places, this was the first time she had gone along. At some places, like Misiones, it was rather hard on her, but she made it and was glad to have had at least one chance to see part of Brazil and the scenic Misiones.

Back from this Misiones-Brazil trip, we had to catch up on correspondence, get material ready for the *Herold* and meet with my colleagues about the status of the work in Entre Rios.

There were changes in the churches, shifts of pastors and installation of new ones. Two ministers from Brazil, Spittler and Reich, were given parishes in Entre Rios, and shortly after, also Ludwig Serfas. These additions gave Entre Rios a real boost.

A church cannot progress very well with only periodic services. Only one church in Entre Rios, Urdinarrain, had services once a month. The other churches had services every six weeks, others every two months, four months and, in the case of Misiones, the pastor appeared twice a year. But in spite of this infrequent coming to the churches, they prospered. They felt the pastor and the church people were of one accord. The people had the freedom of expression and participated in all church governmental affairs.

With so many of our young people moving into Buenos Aires to work, and in many cases, entire families moving there, we began occasional preaching services there, in the church of the Disciples of Christ. By the time we left for the States, we had a number of churches in Buenos Aires.

Reverend Kuhn had left Argentina a year before and in his place came Reverend O. J. Tiede and his wife. The Tiedes stopped in Brazil for a few months before coming to Argentina to get acquainted with the work there, since he was to become the superintendent after my leaving Argentina.

The first duty of Mr. Tiede was to get acquainted with the field in Entre Rios, so the two of us made the rounds of the churches.

He made a very good impression as an elderly man. He and his wife made their home in Concordia where we lived. Concordia subsequently also became the location of our seminary, which was established by Mr. Tiede. In his earlier days in the States, Mr. Tiede taught and, for a short time, also was president of Redfield College and, with this rich experience in education, was a valuable man as my successor in Argentina.

The time was also now at hand for me and my family to get ready to leave for the States. My six-year contract was running out and there was so much to plan and to do before leaving.

We were now six in the family and I agreed with the Mission Committee that I would pay my own fare back to the States. To travel with six in the family over land and sea was a serious matter. Our savings were few, but our faith was strong. The plan was to leave by ship from Buenos Aires to New York and from there by bus to Turtle Lake, North Dakota, to see the parents of my wife. To travel means to learn to pack and to pack properly and swiftly. This we learned. For six years in Argentina, I lived out of my suitcase.

Staying in a foreign country for six years, one also accumulates many costly items. With my trips to other countries in South America, I found many valuable souvenirs that had to be taken along at all costs.

Our children, except the youngest, who was only about a year old, were of great help to us. They spoke Spanish well, keeping up the English too. We considered ourselves a happy family, coming home now with this great experience that all of us had. Certainly we felt this experience would come to good advantage in the many years ahead, and it did. The children did not suffer having moved from school to school and, in addition, learning new languages.

We boarded the ship in Buenos Aires. It was a beautiful sunny afternoon, July 4th, the birthday of our eldest daughter, Grace. We had taken a carriage to the port. Our many pieces of baggage had already been loaded. With a little time on our hands at the port, talking to friends, we noticed that our son had forgotten his overcoat in the school. "I am going to get it," he said and, with that, he started running—he knew the way well. We thought, too, that he would make it, only the traffic worried us. The passengers had already begun to embark, as the captain read off their names.

When our name came, we said, "We are awaiting our son, who had to go back to pick up a forgotten item." Our eyes were always on the direction where our son should come from.

The passengers were now all in the ship and the captain looked at us, wondering what to say—or expecting us to say something. He said, "There is a possibility that he could catch up with us in a private boat."

"Oh, no," we said.

He looked at his watch and said: "I will give you five minutes more."

I began to run in the direction our son would come from, and amid the traffic, I saw him in the distance, running as fast as his legs could carry him. We met and together raced to the port. The sailors were ready to pull the gangplank when the passengers from above shouted, "There they are, hurray!" Puffing and steaming, we boarded the ship and anchors were lifted, then we steamed full speed ahead toward the United States.

On the ship, there was now plenty of time to relax. For diversion, there were games to play, such as table tennis, shuffle board, swimming and entertainment. There was always plenty and a great variety of food for those who did not get sea-sick. I always have been a good eater in my day, except when I am on board a ship, then I am a conservative eater, but not by choice. My family, however, does not have difficulty on board ship. How I have envied them! Here was all this wonderful food to enjoy, but in my case, only to feed the fish!

We had the great pleasure of having with us on the ship Mr. Arturo Toscanini and his orchestra, and Dr. John R. Mott, a noted clergyman and author of many books, who had boarded in Argentina. In Rio de Janeiro, we had a lengthy stop. Most of the passengers got off to see the beautiful city. In this city, each one looks out for himself on the streets. The car drivers are not concerned about the safety of the pedestrians. They are on their own. After leaving Rio, we could observe some sadness in the Toscanini orchestra. It turned out later that one of the members of the orchestra was killed in a streetcar accident. The information of this accident was not brought to the attention of Mr. Toscanini until later on the trip.

Another event on the ship set the passengers into fear everytime it happened. Periodically on the high seas, the ship would zig-zag for many miles, to evade the German submarines prowling the seas. Otherwise, the trip on the boat was restful. We arrived in New York on July 25, the birthday of our second daughter, Margie.

Only those who have lived in a foreign country for some time will appreciate and understand what I am about to say. To live for six years in a country of poor transportation and few comforts of life, especially with a family, brings back thoughts of home, the land of freedom and convenience. To sleep with two to six others in hotels, never sure of your life, eating in the country farms where the farmer has as many as twenty-five horses and as many cows, and no screens on doors and windows, you never know how many flies you have eaten with the meal. In the summer especially, when the insects were in swarms, eating was no pleasure. Sleeping in comfortable beds, you often had many partners, such as fleas, bugs and mosquitoes. One day when I came home from a distant trip, my wife asked: "Did you have a fight?" My forehead still had a big swelling from a black bug the size of a thumbnail. Or take the polverinos, so small that you could hardly see them, that fly by quiet moonlit nights, just taking the joy out of your life. On a short trip to a nearby church, Mrs. Gross and the baby went along. We had to stay overnight in the hotel to go home by train the next day. During the night in the hotel, I awoke from sleep, and went over to see if the child was all right. When I saw her, I called Mrs. Gross, saying, she must have measles. It turned out to be "just" mosquito bites. I could write a fair-sized book on just the behavior of fleas. Fleas everywhere, on the train, in bed — everywhere, these pesty friends are with you.

In the field of business and government, or politics, the story is such that one too had many thoughts of home. The stores are really "open" shops. You can see everything that is for sale in stark display, not wrapped, such as dried cereals, dried fruit, noodles and so on. The sanitary conditions leave much to be desired. The meat market took the prize, at least the first year we were there (in Urdinarrain). The meat market was an open framework with the two halves of the carcasses hanging or suspended from the ceiling. If you did not come with a dish, paper or just a hook, the butcher would wrap it in newspaper, and home you went. In our day, most of the people came with a hook and, thus, walked home from the butcher shop. By now, all of this has changed, of course.

Politics were always interesting to watch. They had a two-party system like in this country. The party members, however, each voted in a different building. The candidate for an office, a high office especially, would, on the night before, arrange a barbecue with plenty of asado (meat) and wine, inviting whoever would come. By the time the party was over, most of them would be voting for him the next day. I actually saw this happen in a little city where I had a church. The different party members would also wear different color caps to distinguish them from one another. There were many clashes between the political party members; clashes not in words, but fists and knife clashes.

Whenever I see a Model A Ford, I want to sit in it, and just reminisce. With the bad roads, the Model A became my best friend. It had a high clearance, was economical and easily repaired. One Sunday, preaching in a nearby church, my plans were to drive home after the afternoon prayer meeting, in order to take the early train to Formosa. Over the noon hour, it began to rain, raining in torrents. I thought of my way back to Concordia and the creek I had to cross. Would I get back in time for the next day's train north? After the prayer meeting, I started out with my friend, the Model A. Sliding back and forth on the road, I finally came to the creek and found the water running quite high. The soil around the area, however, was sandy. I knew the bottom of the creek was solid, but how high was the water I had to cross? To find out, I waded in and found the water coming up to my midriff. I decided to risk it. To make sure the motor would not stop on me, I loosened the fan belt, plugged the oil intake, hung a sack in front of the radiator, and drove across the creek, the motor still running. With a sigh of relief, and with the hope of making it home, I drove off, singing and thanking my Maker for my courage and His help.

Being of an adventurous nature and enjoying frontier life, I and the whole family longed to be back in the land of endless possibilities.

The moment of arrival in New York was here. Many people at the shore waved and shouted, "Welcome home!" All faces were happy faces. Just as soon as the passengers landed, I saw several, myself included, falling prostrate on the ground to kiss it. At last, at home in the land of the free!

Going through Customs is not only time-consuming, it is also a frustrating process. We had about seven large and heavily packed trunks and suitcases. The customs quarters were very large and the crowd in the thousands. In close proximity to us, I noticed the agent requesting a passenger (a movie star) to empty her trunk, down to the last item. I wondered, why? Later, I was told many tourists came back with many highly expensive purchases, trying to work them through the Customs without paying the required duty.

If they will do this to those with a few pieces of luggage, what will they do with ours? Coming from a six-year's stay in Argentina, I thought of the many souvenirs we had accumulated from different countries through the years. A man, unknown to us, came to me and said: "I will help you get through the customs with no charge."

The customs officer walked toward us, looked us over and said: "You are a missionary, from which country are you coming?" After we told him when, where and how, he said: "You may go."

I turned around to look for the gentleman who helped us and to thank him, but he had disappeared. May the good Lord have blessed him. Often in our experiences over the six years in South America, we were convinced that faith is the strongest force that would usually take us through. And, again and again, we had to pray for forgiveness, because of the lack of stronger faith.

The bus trip from New York to Turtle Lake, was not a luxury ride. It was inexpensive, but far from comfortable with a family. Traveling day and night for a few days in the bus became a drain on the amount of our patience. The bus trip was not eventful, aside from our observing the scenery which, needless to say, was beautiful in places. Sitting in the back of the bus, where we could be together more than in front, gave us more conveniences, as well as the chance to be in reach of one another whenever the need arose.

We finally arrived in North Dakota. In Bismarck, we changed buses for Turtle Lake, the goal of our journey. We were tired but happy at the same time to be home with Mrs. Gross' parents, Mr. and Mrs. Bastian. It took several days before our belongings came, but we were taken care of now.

The stay with the in-laws had to be brief. Two important matters had to be considered: first, to work out an itinerary to visit many of our churches to give reports of our South America Mission, and second, to prepare, as soon as possible, for a permanent parish to continue my ministry. There was no question about not receiving a "call" from a church, because there were a number of vacancies. Giving talks, sermons and reports of our missionary work would also give me an opportunity to see the vacant churches and thus save time corresponding with them. To actually see the parish meant saving much time.

Having three children of school age, we had to do something about that before I would leave on a speaking trip. We decided to move to Bismarck, North Dakota, a good transportation center and a city with good schools. We immediately rented a basement apartment large enough for our family and not far from the schools. This was a furnished apartment. As yet, we had not purchased any furniture, waiting for that until we had permanently located. The move from Turtle Lake to Bismarck was accomplished in a short time. By this time, I also had most of the itinerary to visit the churches completed. The speaking trip which took me to many of our churches, took about three months. On this tour to visit the churches, I covered several states—the Dakotas, Montana, Colorado, Nebraska, Oklahoma, Texas, Washington, and California.

Lodi, California, was vacant. It was small in numbers and in equipment, but large in potential. Here I spoke and the response was beyond expectation. After the service, the church went into a conference, and before I left, they gave me a call to serve the church. Having a few relatives in the city, I requested one day to think it over, and promised them my answer before leaving Lodi for Bismarck. It was not the size of membership, nor the church building, nor the present spirit between the members which was bad, that attracted me at all. What I saw here was the great potential. I felt, here is a field that would be a challenge to me. And so, I accepted the call. At once, I called my wife at Bismarck, informing her of the acceptance of a call to serve the Lodi Ebenezer Congregational Church, and that I would be home in a week to pack and to move to Lodi, California. The church also had a parsonage, ready to be occupied.

In a week I was back in Bismarck. The children were taken out of school and in a day we were ready to move to Lodi. In a second-hand car, an Oldsmobile, for which I paid twenty-five dollars, having it fixed up a little, the Gross family moved to Lodi, California, pulling a two-wheel trailer behind. All went well until we came through a town in Montana when a tire on the trailer gave out. Disconnecting the trailer and letting the family stay with the trailer, I drove back to town to buy a tire, taking the old one with me to get the right kind. We lost about two hours, because of the scarcity of that particular kind of tire. We did not mind any inconvenience on this trip, because it went to our new field of pastoral work, and especially, because the field was in California. The rest of the way was done in good time and we arrived in Lodi on November 9, 1940.

The church people had no knowledge of the date of our coming; hence, no one was there to greet us. The parsonage was behind the church, but was locked. It took me only a few minutes to open a window and gain access to the door inside. The parsonage now open, we moved right in and made ourselves at home.

It took only about half an hour before several of the church members, seeing the pastor had arrived, came to help us unload what we had brought with us in the car and on the trailer.

The parsonage had three bedrooms and a study. For this size parsonage, we were very grateful. There was no yard, however, but the children could play across the street on the school grounds. The church was just one large frame building, no classrooms, no study, no narthex; a chancel, yes, but that was all. The membership was "somewhat" divided into two factions, each one trying now to outdo the other in getting close to the pastor. I noticed at once that real diplomacy needed to be applied and without much loss of time. Changes in a new field are always more successful in the first two years of a pastor's ministry in a church.

What I noticed in this church immediately was the good will of the people and the steady church attendance. Old wounds caused before my coming began to heal. The beginning was hard, I admit. On the first Sunday, the Sunday school offering was seventy-five cents. One teacher taught the German "ABC's" and another man taught the class for all the rest, young and old. The beginning could not have been more meager. Yet, I saw through all a yearning for a better church and a will to succeed.

The church attendance increased from Sunday to Sunday. New members joined the church and old dropouts returned. The suggested program was accepted and all I had to do was to lead. It soon became quite apparent that we needed more space, especially classrooms. We needed a basement under the church for the classrooms, as well as two rest-rooms and a study in the church. Before the first year was over, we had started an eight-thousand-dollar building project, providing just the mentioned additions to the old one-room frame church building. I wrote Dr. H. H. Gill, the conference minister at the time, for counsel and approval. By the time he came to Lodi to look over the situation, the church was already on stilts and the full basement practically dug out. I can still see the glow on his face over the sudden and determined activity of the church. Many times later in his reports to the churches, he referred to the Lodi project.

With the new arrangement, we were able to work effectively to provide the members a real church program. The church grew in membership and in many activities. We had two choirs, an orchestra, ladies' organizations, and we undertook many projects as a church. The choirs would alternate in singing on Sundays. The high-school choir, at one time, was twenty-seven members strong. Our own children were a great help in this ministry.

The old factions were soon disappearing with the joining of new members and with the active program of the church. With the new faces and the added new talents of the many who joined, the church just had to grow. We soon found ourselves again with the problem of space. In the Sunday morning service, not only were all the pews filled, but people stood along the wall aisles, sat on the chancel around the pastor and the little ones sat on the chancel floor, facing the people. Something had to be done. Build, we must, but how and where? The fiber of the church people is always put to a test in a building project. This was the case here too. Some just did not want to relocate. To relocate always means more cost, they thought. A special meeting was called and we finally decided to relocate.

We purchased six lots with many fruit trees on it, an old house (furnished), machinery and tools and a couple of engines that the former owner used for cultivations. This land we bought for ten thousand dollars. We engaged Mr. Bissell, from Stockton, to draw us some preliminary plans of a modern church with all the needed rooms for a membership of four hundred. The building committee met with him periodically.

In the meantime, we planned our financial program. The Building Society gave a ten-thousand-dollar grant and a ten-thousand-dollar loan. This was in 1946. Today, the church is free of all indebtedness, and they even paid off the grant. The church was to cost, then, about one-hundred-twenty-thousand dollars, no small amount for a church in those days. We had a goodly number of financially able members. It is my experience, however, that the large sums do not always come from the very rich, but from the many willing ones. This was the case in Lodi, too.

First, we had to dispose of the old house and what was in it, of the machinery and other miscellaneous items, all of which was to bring us needed financial help, aside from the pledges.

Just to show the spirit of this enterprise, especially of the young and middle-aged members, we staged an auction sale, of everything but the old house, for which a good friend offered more than what we would have asked for—one-thousand-three-hundred dollars. We agreed for the rest to be sold to the highest bidder. This auction sale was to bring us not only good financial returns, but also much fun in showing that money-raising could be a pleasure.

The turnout for the auction was excellent. The auctioneer had a sense of humor too, and detected a willing bidder at a glance. There were sundry items for sale, of little value and old, but everything had to be sold. An item that had a value of a dollar was sold for five dollars; an item that might be sold for six dollars, went up to twenty-five dollars. To bid one another up was the aim of all of us, and it certainly created an atmosphere of friendly rivalry for a good cause. The sundry items in the house and yard of this new location cost us three hundred dollars and we sold them for twelve hundred. Many times later in our organization meeting, we would talk about this wonderful auction sale and the good spirit it developed.

The church had a good standing in the community, and I was also active in the community, as a member of the Lion's Club, the Local Legion Post (chaplain) and I managed the newly organized

Service Center, which was a project of the Ministerial Association. The church had put on many dinners and developed a reputation for serving good dinners. The people would come to eat here far and wide.

The finance committee was a very active one, contacting not only the membership, but also the people in the community. I was asked to be of help in raising money. Needless to say, I had the time of my life. I enjoyed it. There were big sums and little sums coming in. There were large and small pledges, to be sure, during the time the church was being built. To show the spirit of the people toward this building project, I mention with great joy how several working couples, with no savings, and with families to rear and educate, would go to the bank and borrow hundreds of dollars on a note, just to be a part of this building project.

There was another case of a nonmember, a funeral director, a good friend of mine, to whom I went and said: "Harry, I have a bill here. I would like to have you take care of it." The bill was for six hundred dollars for the purchase of the art windows that were replaced by stained glass windows at the chapel of the College of the Pacific (now Pacific University).

Harry pulled a desk-drawer, reached for his checkbook, looked at me and said: "OK, Fred, I will gladly take care of the bill." This incident was duplicated many times during the financial drive.

Lest one get the impression, however, that the financial drive was one hundred percent-plus, let me say there was a small group of incorrigibles who saw only the dark side of this building project and, therefore, did everything possible to hinder the cause. As indicated earlier, building a church brings out of a man his true attitude, which does not mean the minority or the opposition is always wrong, but there is a difference between being against and undermining the majority and, often times, resorting to low means, such as character assassination tactics.

The Lodi church was a yoked church when I accepted the call; it was yoked with the Elk Grove church, which church received the pastor every third Sunday. After about a year in Lodi, the church demanded the pastor full time and asked the Elk Grove church to apply for a pastor to serve them. (Later, more of the Elk Grove church.)

As the membership grew and more organizations in the church

were established, so also grew the interest in the church. This interest had to be harnessed into good channels of services. To do this, two special projects were accepted for the church; one, to have an annual Mission Sunday, at which time an outside speaker was engaged to deliver sermons on the Cause of Missions and to accept special offerings at each service; the other project was an annual bazaar with a dinner, also once a year.

On Mission Day Sunday the members were always asked weeks before to be prepared and to help make the day a sacrificial success. Through the years, the German background churches followed this practice of Mission Day services with continued success. For us, Mission Day was, therefore, a special day and a day not to be taken lightly. On this day, all moneys, from worship services and the offering of the Sunday school, all went to missions. The different organizations of the church would contribute annually a special amount out of their treasury toward the total sum on Mission Day. In this church and many others of our German-speaking churches, the Mission-giving amounted to as much as three thousand dollars each, on one day. The Lodi church, too, had offerings on Mission Day, as much as twenty-four hundred dollars.

The other project was the annual bazaar, for which the members would prepare during the year, by sewing and quilting on the part of the ladies, and making things, such as toys, little stools, racks, tables, et cetera—all for the bazaar in the fall of the year. Sometimes, a business church member would donate an item from his store for this cause.

The ladies of the church, with the help of the men, planned a good dinner for the bazaar, invited the public and charged a nominal amount for the ticket. The auction sales at the bazaar were usually a success, due to people bidding more than an item was worth. I remember several occasions when a quilt went as high as one hundred dollars. Why? It was for the church. The dinners, by this time, had the reputation of being the best dinners served in town. People would come from distant places because of the good food. To this day, this church, annually, clears as much as two thousand dollars in one night just from the dinner. Needless to say, it took a lot of hard work and cooperation.

One may be tempted to say, "What about the spiritual life of the church?" One really has a right to ask such a question. People can be brought to cooperate and to work for the church but, invariably, before one can get a church to work hard, there must be a motive, a cause, an objective. There has to be a motivating spirit within us before we can reach out to affect others. The secret, of course, is not hard to pinpoint.

Another practice of our South-Russia-German forefathers, was an annual Evangelistic meeting of two to eight weeks' duration, depending upon the results of the meetings.

This pietistic spirit of our forefathers was practiced in southern Germany, continued in Russia and brought to this country. The church agreed on the date of meetings to be held and designated the speaker to lead the meetings. The meetings took place nightly and sometimes in the daytime for those who were not occupied with singing, preaching and praying on the knees, until a person felt his sins were forgiven and he was accepted by Christ. As related earlier regarding Hebron, North Dakota, here, too, hundreds made their confession public and were now committed to Christ. Such experiences are the spiritual harvesttimes for a church.

When such commitments take place, the church has the motive and the secret to cause the church to work and grow. They have found a reason for reaching out to help others. The committed men and women have now the love of Christ, the greatest thing in the world to motivate them. Love, however, to be sustained, must always have an object, otherwise it is not love.

Whatever one thinks of these evangelistic meetings, and however one might interpret them, one thing is sure: man is no more as he was. Now, all things are new. "A new creation," as Paul says.

The church-building project was finally finished and the church dedicated in 1946. There was much donated help from members and nonmembers. The professional workers worked for a reduced hourly wage. Older people did lighter work. Once the building was in progress, even some of the incorrigibles showed up and began to smile over the progress of the church. I, too, spent hours upon hours on this church project. I feel I know every inch of that church. I had the time of my life, both in actual physical work, as well as in approaching people for donations. In fact, the rumor went around for people to hide their money and their silverware when Fred Gross came around! We now saw our way clear. Financially, the goal would be reached. It was hope, hard work, and cooperation that did it.

The first ceremony in the very-soon-completed building project was the Raising of the Cross, with Dr. Breed of our Stockton church as the guest preacher. Very few people had ever witnessed such a ceremony. The service was held outside, with a good view of the tower, and the people gathered around an improvised platform. The carpenters who made the cross were high up on the tower, dressed in white overalls and, with rope in hand, hoisted the cross on high, while the audience sang, "In the Cross of Christ I Glory." It was a moving experience, to say the least. For weeks after, the people talked about this service.

On the day of dedication, the church was filled to capacity. It holds, with the balcony, about five hundred people. The narthex was filled and many stood outside. A sound-system brought the words to those outside. The people first gathered outside the main entrance of the church. The pastor opened the service and then, with the singing of the hymn, "Tut mir auf die schoene Pforte.." (Open wide the gates of Heaven), the procession into the church took place until all seats were filled, the rest having to stand around the open windows and, thus, also becoming part of the worshipping group.

Dr. Harley H. Gill, Superintendent of the Northern California Conference of Congregational Churches, was the preacher. With characteristic sincerity and biblical preaching, he succeeded in bringing the congregation to a genuine spirit of worship. It was a great day for the church, the denomination, and the community. Personally, I felt this was the high point in my ministry in this country.

On June 20, 1948, the cornerstone-laying service was held and in November of 1948, the church was dedicated.

Two times in my ministry, my church hosted the German Congregational Conference; in Hebron, North Dakota in 1932, and in Lodi, in June of 1947. It was always considered an honor for the pastor and the church to be able to host the general conference, because of the tremendous undertaking and sacrifice it usually required. Building churches has also been looked upon as a great achievement. The Lodi church built and enlarged its church facilities twice and once hosted the general conference. This was an achievement and an honor.

The Lodi Ebenezer Congregational Church was considered one of the most beautiful churches in the city. It was referred to as "the church of the quiet beauty." Requests came from several pastors for pictures or cuts of the church and left-over plans by the architect for them to study.

Mr. Howard G. Bissell, Architect, of Stockton, California, submitted the following write-up of the Lodi Church:

THE ARCHITECTURE OF THE EBENEZER CONGREGATIONAL CHURCH, Lodi, California.

"In briefly summarizing the type of plan and style of architecture which were the goal of the architect and builders in the design of the Ebenezer Congregational Church of Lodi, one is tempted to delve into the History of Christian Church Architecture. This takes us back to the Early Christian times of the century in ancient Rome, where a so-called Basilican type of church plan found its earliest expression. Fundamentally a Basilican plan is an oblong type of church plan with nave and side aisle, and aisle walls, with either of two types of construction: both nave and side aisles placed under one roof; or the nave raised in height to clerestory or higher window looking over the roof over the side aisle. An example of the latter is found in the Chapel of the College of the Pacific, while the former is illustrated by the Ebenezer Congregational Church.

We must pass down through the centuries of Christendom during which the Basilica developed in the plan and construction through the complications of design found in the Romanesque and Gothic styles, as illustrated in the larger churches and cathedrals of Europe and England, offering, with amplications, the Basilican plan. "The history of Gothic Architecture in England" as told by Francis Bond, elaborates at length on the various design and plan elements of the Romanesque and Gothic churches in England which have influenced the architecture of the church down to our time.

Along with the construction of the great cathedrals of England, there was developed from earlier ecclesiastical forms the parish church which eventually assumed a Basilican type of plan. The parish church has often been regarded as a simplified off-shoot of the great cathedral plan, but actually it was an amplification of its own earlier and humbler Anglo-Saxon form. Historically there developed several types of English parish churches, thousands of which were built, both great and small, in Anglo-Saxon, Norman and later Gothic phases of architectural history.

The Ebenezer Congregational Church may be said to be a modernized version and adaptation of the English Parish Church of the so-called fifth type, having the aisles nave, the partially aisled chancel and screened narthex, all under one roof. The width and length of the nave and of the balcony were indicated by the seating capacity desired by the Ebenezer Congregation, but the plan is essentially a Basilican plan. The architectural separations between the chancel, the nave and the balcony have been achieved by the slightly pointed plaster arches, while the main wide roof spans both nave and the side aisles. Although structural requirements led to the use of steel trusses, unknown of course in earlier days, these have been concealed by architecturally framed purloins and sloping beams, between which a finished ceiling of insulating materials has been placed for acoustical purposes. In plan the center nave aisle continues from the narthex to the altar in the chancel, with the pulpit and lectern on either side, the choir stalls divided, and the organ console behind the altar.

With regard to the tower design and location, the typical parish Church would have placed this architectural element on the center line of the nave, either over a center vestibule, over the center of the narthex, or over a crossing located between the nave and the chancel. In such cases the tower was necessarily supported in its construction from the ground up through the nave roof, and had to be of such height as to dominate the entire church. In many cases, however, particularly in a generally Gothic design, a more formal type of plan located the tower off center, and over an entrance vestibule adjacent to the narthex at one end.

With problems of general design and plan in mind, as well as the costs of construction, the planning of the Ebenezer Congregational Church placed the tower over the vestibule at the junction between the main church and the other elements required for the complete church plant. Located thus off center, and designed in a simplified type of Gothic tower architecture, the tower with its spire is sufficient to dominate the entrance in perspective, and at the same time permit the eastern chancel gable wall with its Gothic window to achieve its own importance. The tower distinctly indicates the main entrance vestibule. From this vestibule and adjacent narthex, access is had to all the other departments of the church, such as Prayer and Social Rooms, Parlor, Sunday School Rooms, Kitchen and other service elements. From the narthex, stairs lead to the second floor and other rooms for educational and social purposes, as well as to the balcony.

The planners of the Ebenezer Congregational Church thus attempted to include all the various elements of the complete church plant in a unified whole, while adhering to the best traditions of the English Parish Church with such modifications as to structure, plan and design as seemed desirable to meet the needs of this congregation, but without sacrificing certain architectural principles.

Howard G. Bissell
Architect
September, 1948

The above description of the architectural design of the Ebenezer Congregational Church is a rather lengthy one, but I felt it necessary to have it included in this book, for posterity and for the sake of record.

After the completion of the church and especially since the dedication brought hundreds to come and see the church, many compliments from far and near were heard, praising the church and its pastor for this venture in faith to build a church of such magnitude. None of these compliments and praises pleased me more than the one by the superintendent, Dr. Gill, who was always a great inspiration to me, and especially during the process of construction of the church. I will quote Dr. Gill's letter herewith:

Rev. Fred W. Gross
515 So. Garfield St.,
Lodi, California

My dear Mr. Gross:

Mrs. Gill and I are still under the spell of last Sunday. It was a magnificently planned day, and the response of the Lodi people was revealing. We still cannot see how you ever did it. I have seen great buildings erected on a shoe-string, but I cannot remember having seen such a building so nearly covered financially. You are entitled to great credit. More than that, what has been accomplished is a testimony to the centrality of the Gospel of Christ in the hearts of your people.

We thank your church for the fine dinner, and we thank you for giving us the opportunity to have a part in the service.

Your sincere friend,
Harley H. Gill.

After serving the Lodi church for eight and a half years, considering how much was accomplished, I began to feel my work was done, and looked around for another church which might be in need of me. Throughout my ministry, I felt that the minister should leave a church while the leaving is in good spirit. To out-stay one's welcome runs the church down and does no good to the minister.

Serving the Ebenezer Church for eight and a half years, I brought the membership from seventy-five up to over four hundred and built a new $125,000 church, was chaplain of the American Legion for ten years, and member of the Lions Club for eight years. Thus, I thought I had left a positive imprint upon the community.

Ministers often say among themselves, "No matter how well things might go in a church, when you build a church and have completed the project, you will have to leave the church." This was also true in my case. I do not consider it to be regretful. On the contrary, it is wise to leave a church when people still think well of you.

Thus, I resigned in February of 1949, hoping to receive a call from another church.

A German saying, interpreted, meaning, "Man thinks, but God guides," was also true in my case here in Lodi and many times since.

When my resignation from the church became known in the community, many influential Lodi citizens prevailed upon me to stay in the community and, to hold me, they would establish for me an office as "community counselor," with offices in the City Hall. The city and the schools got together and agreed to share the budget of this office. After accepting this new full-time office, I was assigned a room in the city hall, equipped according to my wishes, and given not only a good salary, but also a more-than-adequate budget for books and supplies. My responsibilities were to be the city manager. Periodically, I gave a written report to the city fathers.

After church in Entre Rios. An outdoor Sunday service.

A guitar orchestra in Rio Granda do Sul Church, Brazil.

A couple getting married in Entre Rios, Argentina.

Transportation in Brazil.

Reverends Kuhn, Liede, Geier, Gross, and Sertas, pastors in Argentina and Brazil, 1936-1940.

A confirmation class in Entre Rios.

Horses of a large-scale farmer in Entre Rios.

Out-of-door cooking and baking in the Chaco, Argentina.

Building a home in Entre Rios.

A typical farm in Entre Rios.

Chapter 20
THE COUNSELING YEARS IN LODI

In bringing about this new office of counseling in Lodi, a special role was played by the local American Legion Post, of which I was chaplain for many years. The Legion had a very good reputation in the whole Lodi district and beyond, largely due to the effective military funerals we conducted and also because some of the most influential men of the community were Legionnaires. Through the years, I had done private counseling and, in a few cases, even for people beyond the community. Now, however, I was to have complete freedom and the equipment to do a good job of full-time counseling to all in need.

My office was advertised in the local papers and also over TV through the Stockton station. This brought to me people from all walks of life, from nearby as well as distant places. I cooperated with the County Juvenile Office and also with the Welfare Department. The ministers of the community referred many cases to me, as did the schools. My name, "Fred," became a household word.

To become more familiar with the art of counseling, I attended the many societies, county and state, that dealt with human relations. The budget even allowed me to attend C.O.P. in Stockton, specializing in child psychology and play-therapy. Churches, schools, clubs, P.T.A.'s and even colleges invited me to give talks about my work.

I enjoyed my work thoroughly. Although I had office hours, people would call me any time of the day and night. I did not mind it, feeling that if people are desperate, I should be ready to serve. I received a questionnaire once, which asked the question, "Do you confine your counseling strictly to your office?" No, not at all. I counseled wherever and whenever a person approached me for counsel, be it in my office, my study, in the church, on the street, on the ball-field, between the stacks of the grocery store, in the car or in the homes.

The counseling cases were of every imaginable type, even some of an unthinkable nature. They were also found on any level of society. Cases came to me from as far as a hundred and two hundred miles away. All cases could not be treated alike. To be fair, I gave each case about an hour's time. It could not, however, be a hard and fast rule, for some people are talkative, others are reserved. In one case, I had to give the person two hours a week and she would still, in the meantime, send me a two-page typewritten letter. This person just needed more time to talk herself out.

My knowledge of play-therapy was of invaluable help to me. In the corner of my room, I had quite an assortment of toys and games, clay, pencils, crayons and some sharp items, such as knives and pokes, all to observe the youngster in what he might show the most interest. Often I would let him draw or write down his dreams. It is amazing to see what comes out of a person who is troubled.

Probably it would be better if I would let someone else speak about my work in Lodi. In the November 26, 1954 issue of *Collier's* magazine, Mr. John Wesley Noble wrote the following:

TOWN TROUBLE SHOOTER

People with problems in Lodi, California take them to Fred Gross. Officially, he's a public counselor, but more often he's turned to as a neighbor and friend.

Every town has its troubles, the troubles of its citizens. And people with problems need an understanding listener. It is a simple need, but often difficult to satisfy; private counseling may be expensive and mental health agencies frequently are tied up in more red tape than troubled people have the time to cut. Many towns, realizing the need for fast, direct contact between a troubled mind and a sympathetic ear, have sought and found short cuts to mental health. Lodi, California is one such town.

If you live in Lodi, and you've got troubles, you go to see Fred Gross. Gross, fifty-nine, is an ordained Congregational minister—and he is also the town's trouble shooter. He is known, officially, as Counselor: Lodi Counseling Center.

Gross's office has no prescribed term of service: its current annual cost of $7,707, which includes his salary and expenses, is covered jointly by the city and school-system budgets; and its facilities are available gratis to the 14,000 residents of Lodi and some 35,000 ranchers and farmers in neighboring areas. The facilities specifically: common sense and a willing ear.

Fred Gross has been looking for trouble since 1948, when Lodi first created his office to stem a rising tide of juvenile delinquency. What was needed, Lodi decided at a town meeting, was someone to whom the youngsters and their parents could talk to freely. No social workers, no police reports, no red tape—just a friend with wisdom, patience and understanding.

Gross was picked for the job because, in the eight years in residence in Lodi, he had counseled widely and successfully in and out of his church. People knew him and people trusted him. So the town gave him an office in city hall and told him to go to work.

In his first year as public counselor Gross scotched delinquency so effectively, through parent-and-child interviews, constant personal guidance and school-organized programs, that his services were spontaneously extended well beyond delinquents into every kind of adult problem, from the minor snags of everyday living to situations requiring long-term psychiatric aid.

The last, Gross refers to specialists. But more often he does the job himself, listening, questioning, advising, turning occasionally to the pile of psychology texts he keeps in his office, and always to his own store of practical wisdom.

He attends P.T.A. meetings, works for the Salvation Army, runs an informal employment agency for high-school graduates, and invites panels of experts into Lodi to lecture on jobs, sex and marriage. Wherever trouble is a potential, Fred Gross goes after it. Because, as he says: "Leave it alone, and it will ripen into tragedy."

And Lodi is finding, as are other towns with similar solutions, that a common-sense supplement to conventional counseling can stop a lot of trouble.

—John Wesley Noble.

My services as community counselor in Lodi lasted for four and a half years. They were years of excellent services, more so than can be expressed in words. Many came to say, "You saved my life." Or others, "What you have done for my son cannot be paid in money."

In spite of all the success and the good will toward me, the time also came for me to quit this office. The reason? A new police chief from out-of-state was appointed. In time, he began to come to my office for some information about certain youngsters. I gave him only such information that would not betray the confidence the youngsters had in me. In time, however, he insisted that I completely open my files to him. "That," I said, "I cannot do." But, he insisted and finally persuaded the majority of the city fathers to help him get his way. The vote was four to three in his favor. With this attitude, I handed in my resignation as community counselor of Lodi, California.

There were many influential citizens in the community who wanted me to fight the action of the city fathers, but I did not want to see the city divided and an ill feeling among themselves created, just to force the issue. Succeeding years would not have been happy ones.

I never had to beg for a position in my life and I felt this would also be the case after leaving this job. In fact, the next job had already come to me, before I quit the counseling office in Lodi.

The F.W. Gross family in Argentina, 1942.

Our son, Vernon, in the school uniform, Entre Rios.

Ebenezer Congregational Church, Lodi, California.

Chapter 21

THE ELK GROVE CHURCH

The Elk Grove Congregational Church was yoked with the Lodi church, receiving services every third Sunday. In about two years, the Lodi church, having grown fast in membership, demanded that I serve them full-time. Elk Grove was then served by a retired pastor, Reverend John F. Reister, and a couple years later by a minister, Reverend F. C. Zahl, who, to make ends meet, also worked in a grocery store. Some time before I quit the Lodi office, he accepted a call from Medina, North Dakota.

Elk Grove then approached me to serve them and, having my Sundays free, while still counseling in Lodi, I accepted the request to serve Elk Grove. At this time, Elk Grove was still a German-speaking church, realizing, however, that a change would have to be made soon. In fact, my immediate predecessor indicated to me that the church in Elk Grove had no future and gave it about two more years before it folded.

We called a meeting of the Elk Grove membership (about twenty-two families) to discuss the future of the church. The church was a one-room frame building in an old section of town. The parsonage of the church, however, was in good condition and was large enough for a family with children. The members of the church were very much concerned about the future of their church. They realized the strikes against them: they were a German preaching church with very few German-speaking people left in the community; and the present location of the church was a very poor one. Although I was chairman of the meeting, I felt I needed to be cautious, not to make too many suggestions to begin with, but simply to guide them. When a business lady of the church made the suggestion to discontinue the German services, I thought this was a good beginning. There was silence for a moment. I knew what it meant for the elderly people to have the services in English. Soon others joined in the idea of having English services, realizing that the whole future of the church was dependent upon it. A charter member of the church directed the question to me, saying, "Pastor, how do things look to you?"

I said: "I agree that we have a future only by starting to have English services." There seemed to be total agreement on this point.

Now the question was: "What about relocating?" The discussion began on a low key—not that the will to relocate was lacking but, there were questions: how? where? and when? I sensed that now was the time for me to speak. I had thought about the Elk Grove church many times, having served it eight years earlier. I had definite plans to suggest to the members, who valued my judgment. I said, "It can be done, if we cooperate and are willing to sacrifice." My plan was as follows: to sell the church and parsonage, take pledges, buy lots at a certain area (where the church is now), and then go full speed ahead.

There were no objections to my plan but, I am sure, many thought to themselves, "I hope it will work." It was now up to me; that I also knew.

The parsonage was already rented and had a prospective buyer. Still serving Lodi as counselor, I had only some evenings to myself and always Sundays. (Many business meetings were held on Sundays.) We knew the owner of the lots we wanted, at the choicest location in Elk Grove. The church treasurer and I drove to Sacramento one night to negotiate the purchase of six lots. It was midnight by the time we got back, but the deal for the six lots was made to the satisfaction of both the seller and buyer.

But the major task, that of money, was still to be solved. The church had made great strides in the first year I served them full-time. The new program of the church appealed to both old and young. But now, to build a new church, we needed to get the finances. The planning committee suggested to begin small and add as we grew, a thought that appealed to most of the members. We gave our pledges and our cash and found that we had ten thousand dollars to begin with. The lots were paid for. Ten thousand dollars would not build a church, even in those days. The sale of the parsonage brought us fourteen thousand more. (We were still living in our own house in Lodi.)

A certain Mr. Grosz from Kulm, North Dakota, when living in Elk Grove, had purchased for himself two lots next to the old church. He later moved back to the Dakotas again. One day I received a letter from him, saying, "If you sell the lots for me, I will give you a good commission." This letter came to me at just the right time. I made a counter-offer to him and, in my answer to his letter, said: "I have a much better offer to make to you, Mr. Grosz, about your two lots in Elk Grove. Give them to us and let us sell them to help us build a new church in another location."

Months passed, until finally one day, here was a letter from Mr. Grosz with a note: "Rev. Gross, here are the deeds to my lots in Elk Grove, a contribution toward your building project." Another prayer answered, I was sure. And, so it went on and on in the process of building a church from shoe-strings.

Instead of engaging a regular architect and paying him his going fees, I approached the Lodi city engineer, Mr. L. Singer, to draw up the plans for the church, for which he charged us only one hundred dollars. Later, he also supervised the construction, coming up after his working hours in Lodi and also on Saturdays. We were good friends for many years. All other professional help I also got from Lodi, and usually at a reduced charge. In addition, not only did our own members put in hours upon hours of donated labor, but many of my friends in Lodi would come up to help, especially on Saturdays.

The ladies of the church put on dinners and bazaars to increase the amount of the building fund. To make the building story of this church (the first unit) construction short, I can truthfully say that by 1950, the church was dedicated and all bills paid. The cost of the church, not figuring the donated help, came to about forty thousand dollars.

Dr. H. H. Gill, still the conference minister, of course, knew what I was doing and one day, with one of the top officials from New York, came to see the church. This was a week before the dedication, at which dedication Dr. Gill was again the preacher. When Dr. Gill and Dr. North of New York came to Elk Grove, they were looking for the new church. Never having been in Elk Grove before, they inquired and were directed to a new church on the other side of town. When they got there, Dr. North remarked, "This is an architectural monstrosity; Fred Gross does not build a church like that." They drove on and finally came to where our new church was located, entered the church, and paused, saying, "This is more like Fred Gross." They were pleased with what they saw and Dr. Gill remarked, "Fred, you are a church builder!" At the dedication services, people from far and wide filled the little church to capacity. The community people could not understand how it was possible for a language church to make such tremendous progress in a small community. It was done and my church members took on a new lease on life.

This, however, was only the first chapter in the Elk Grove church building project. During all of this time, I was still living in our own home in Lodi, serving Elk Grove on Sundays. With the new church, a special visual aids program was initiated for Sunday nights. That proved a blessing for both old and young. The church grew in membership and the young peoples' work was strong and healthy, by which I mean that the emphasis was on knowing what it meant to be a Christian. We soon had two choirs and never lacked choir leaders or organ players. It soon became evident that we needed a parsonage to have a resident pastor.

With the first unit, the sanctuary, erected, we directed our energy toward a new parsonage. The lots were already purchased. The plans for a parsonage I got from a magazine on houses from the east and, with some modification and help again from Mr. Singer, city engineer of Lodi, an acceptable parsonage plan was accepted by the church. As in the case of the church, so in the case of the parsonage, much help was donated. The parsonage was finished in a few months and then rented for one hundred and twenty-five dollars a month until we would move into it ourselves.

The third unit, the education building, was to be the largest project of the church, located between the church and the parsonage. For this project we engaged an architect from Oakland, California. It was to be a sixty-thousand-dollar project, consisting of a large fellowship hall and two-story classroom sections adjoining the fellowship hall. Would this be possible? No one, however, raised any objections to the erection of this unit. Many times the thought arose in me, "Will you make it this time?" My answer to myself was, as before, "It is the Cause of Christ and I shall not fail."

If I ever had a church with a membership living in harmony and with such dedication to the church, it was Elk Grove. To know this, for me was to know the secret of success. The old members, some of whom were still charter members, (the church was organized in 1923), always encouraged the others to sacrifice to the limit for the cause of Christ. They were church people, some of whom were faithful members from the old country, Russia. Some were farmers, business people, teachers, secretaries, laborers, et cetera; a cross-section of people at work. There were also a few carpenters, one of whom had been a carpenter in Russia, who did all the altar, pulpit and lectern construction of the church.

With the church and the parsonage completed and in the best section of town, we now tackled the hardest unit, for which the money was not yet available. Sixty thousand dollars is a lot of money for a still-modest number of church members. It has, however, been my experience that it is not always the money that builds a church but, rather, the dedication to a cause, in this case to the church. I felt my members had what was needed — a living faith in the Cause of Christ and a commitment to Him who saved them. With this power, I knew we could not fail.

Worshipping now in the new church, the increasing membership took on a new image. At the beginning, this church had only German-speaking members; now, however, non-German-speaking people joined the church. And, this is what we wanted, too. Up to that time, we had been referred to in the community as "The German Church." This now changed. In fact, the time came when we not only had teachers from the schools in our membership, but even a school principal and the district school superintendent. Our church had a good standing in the community.

With all the good will of the members, and the good standing in the community, our hopes to succeed were realized.

The financial drive began, first of all, again by pledges on the part of the members and friends of the church. We knew that in this project we would have to approach the bank for a longer period note. But our financial drive was begun in good tempo. And now living in Elk Grove, I could give full time to my church work, and I loved it. Meeting after meeting was held and plans analyzed as to how to get the most for the money. With my many friends in Lodi and the former members of the Lodi church, I knew we could save money again as we did with the other units.

The church pledges, however, must come first, to show what your own members are willing to do. It has been my experience through the years in the church that if you want to succeed in the church, you must lead with a good example. This is also true with soliciting money for the Cause of Christ. And so in the Elk Grove case, my family pledged one thousand dollars for this third unit, the education building. The business-people members also pledged a thousand each, and so on down to the last member, each made a sacrificial pledge for the church building fund.

Among our newly received church members was a family that periodically brought an elderly woman to church with them. She lived in Sacramento and was the sister of the husband of this family. This lady, Mrs. Gostick, the widow of a doctor who was a former schoolteacher, enjoyed coming to our church, I was informed later, because the pastor had a heart for the young people, and his sermons were sincere. She had no church affiliation, nor did she ever join our Elk Grove church, but her heart was with us and she loved to come to our church in Elk Grove.

After having given all the church members a chance to pledge for the new unit of the church, we also approached the friends of the church, many of whom contributed liberally, including this woman. In fact, she made the first move by inviting me to her home in Sacramento because she wanted to ask me a number of questions about the future of the church.

On the appointed date, I called on her. She was friendly and showed considerable concern about the building project. Having been satisfied with the answers I gave her, she reached for her checkbook and wrote out a three-thousand-dollar check, remarking that, in addition, she would contribute annually in terms of money and in items the church might be in need of. She followed through with this promise of contributing liberally in the future. She later paid for the stained-glass rose window, which cost seven hundred dollars. She paid for the carpeting of the chancel, the church sound system, a piano and many other items the church needed.

I think it would be of interest to read the description of the Rose Window of the church in Elk Grove, as given by the company in San Francisco:

> The new rose window is a symbolic conception, portraying the focal point of the Christian Faith through the medium of glistening color in light. The central motif of our window is the communion cup. This, of course, is the symbol of our Lord

at the Last Supper—"Do this in remembrance of Me." The cup is placed within an aura of blazing light, symbol of Our Lord as the "Light of the World."

In the upper "cusp" of the window we see the monogram "IHC." This is the ancient Greek monogram of the name "Jesus." The "I" (Iota) is our modern "J," the "H" (Eta) is our "E," and the "C" (Sigma) is the Latin "S". Thus, "IHC" is "JES," the first three letters of the Greek "JESOUS." In the lower "cusp" is the ancient Greek monogram for "the anointed one," i.e., "Christos." The "X" (Chi), and the "P" (Rho) is our Latin or English "R." Thus we have "Chr," the first three letters of the Greek word "Christos." In the left and right "cusps" of the window, we see the Greek letters "Alpha and Omega." These are the first and last letters of the Greek alphabet, and are suggested by St. John in Revelations 1:9: "I am Alpha and Omega, the beginning and the end."

In the four corners of the "cusps," we see small representations of four open books. These four books are the "Word," the Gospels of Matthew, Mark, Luke and John.

The entire window is colored in the rich primary hues of ruby, blue and gold, the colors of love, wisdom and majesty. There are interesting secondary accents of turquoise and green, the entire scheme being planned to insure a rich and glittering fabric of light and color that can serve as an inspiration to worship and prayer."

This rose window was an inspiration to many worshippers and the children often remarked about its beauty. The rose window and the liberal monetary contributions of this lady have rooted her in our church. She would never miss a dinner or a bazaar sponsored by our ladies.

The building project of the last unit, the education building, began in full swing. It was the talk of the town. Even charity can become contagious. People are inherently altruistic. A local gravel dealer with no church affiliation, donated all the gravel needed for the parking area of the church. On Saturdays, people we never thought of came to donate their help. Young people, high-school youngsters, too, not members, came to help. With my secondary credential, I, at times, did substitute teaching and became acquainted with the young people of Elk Grove. My counseling work also attracted free labor.

The greatest surprise in the phase of donating free labor came one Saturday when about twelve younger adults came from the Lodi church to lay the shingles. In one day it was completed! It was a pleasure to see these men work. They worked as if it had been their own building. Individually, some of these men came from Lodi at a time they had available. Even my grandson, who happened to be visiting with us, insisted I give him a hammer to help on the roof. It was a pleasing picture to see Tim on the roof with a brand-new hammer I bought him, and joining the others to have a part in building a church.

More than ever before, with the necessary equipment now available to put on large scale public dinners, our ladies enjoyed preparing the annual dinners. As many as fifteen huge turkeys were prepared and hundreds of people served home-style all the food on the table, with everyone eating as much as he could put away. People came to these dinners from as far as Lodi and Sacramento. The men and women of the church cooperated as a unit to put on what otherwise might have meant a necessary chore.

The Education Unit was dedicated, with Dr. Breed of Stockton, California delivering the sermon. Neighboring pastors, also including Dr. Simmons from Sacramento, were here to celebrate with us. The church, at the day of dedication of the last unit, had an indebtedness of about twenty thousand dollars, carried by the Farmers and Merchants Bank of Sacramento, California. From year to year, the church reduced this debt.

While serving the Elk Grove church, I planned to take my first trip to Russia, which I shall report on later.

In 1960, Dr. and Mrs. George Kibbey planned a trip to Hawaii, picking up a car upon arrival. We joined them and stayed ten days. It was a much-needed vacation after so many strenuous months of church activity and also after a hospitalization shortly before.

Rested and encouraged by seeing the many churches at work in the Islands, we came back to renew our efforts in making Elk Grove a going church. The church building is located in the choicest area of town and the whole plant is an imposing group of buildings in the area.

In the fifty years of my ministry, outside of my work in Argentina and Brazil, the Lodi and the Elk Grove churches were the two fields that really challenged my energy and spirit to work for the Cause of Christ—Lodi, from a small membership and a one-room frame building, to building two times, the second time in relocation, and increasing the membership from seventy-five to over four hundred; and the second church, Elk Grove, also with a small membership, worshipping in a one-room frame building in a poor district of town, to a one-hundred-sixty membership church of three units in a very desirable location, surrounded by some of the best residences in Elk Grove—all this was a joy indeed.

To develop a condition and a relationship with people to result in building and enlarging a church plant five times, is reason to be grateful. Someone once said, "It is one thing to bring the people to the church, but something else to keep them in the church." There is much truth in this quotation. To my inner satisfaction, I can truthfully say that the fields I have served in my ministry were always stronger when I left than they were when I came to the field. To see a people grow and take interest in the program of the church, as well as carry on a desirable missionary outreach, are, it seems to me, a good indication of spiritual growth.

To retire from the full-time ministry raises two questions in a minister's life: one, have I been successful in my ministry? and second, what will retirement be like?

The high school choir of the Ebenezer Congregational Church, 1944, directed by Reverend Gross.

Chapter 22

RETIREMENT IN 1962 AND MOVING TO SACRAMENTO, CALIFORNIA

The retirement year for the average minister is sixty-five. In my case, the age was sixty-eight. Secretly, I was in hopes of continuing the ministry, at least part-time. These hopes became realities in a short time.

While still in Elk Grove, we felt it was time to look for a place of retirement and also to purchase a house in a desirable location. We chose to retire in Sacramento, a city we had always liked very much. It was not too large and had many opportunities for retired people. We also hoped to become members of the Pioneer Congregational Church in Sacramento. Thus, we bought a house on 2920 26th Street. This was two years before we retired. In the two years before retirement, our house was rented for $125 a month, which gave us a little capital to do some redecorating before moving into the house ourselves two years later.

Moving into Sacramento was a quick and inexpensive process. The Elk Grove members with several trucks and pick-ups made moving a swift job.

Our home in Sacramento had three bedrooms and a partial basement. One bedroom I used for my study and the basement I used for my hobbies. The Sacramento Senior Citizens' Center between J and I Streets was a good place to learn hobbies. I went there many times and learned copper-plating and stone-work such as making tile chess tables.

Soon, another hobby seemed to have been thrust upon me. Continuing with counseling after retirement, I met a lady artist who came to me for help in keeping her marriage together. To show her gratefulness, she offered me free art lessons. In addition to the free lessons, she also gave me an easel, paint and brushes. I took about six lessons and then had to quit, because the local Pioneer church asked me to become their minister of Counseling and Visitation.

This was the offer I had hoped to get someday, and here it was. With much joy and anticipation, I assumed my new services in a field I felt I had exceptional aptitude in.

This new ministry, with a large membership church and in a big city, was just what I had hoped and prayed for, for a long time. For the time being, I had to quit my latest hobby and concentrate on counseling and calling on people. But the counseling pause did not last very long. Many new cases in the community came to my attention. One case in particular, again a case of an artist, pleaded with me for help with his spouse and, if successful, he would give me all my art lessons free. Here I was. What should I do? My time in the church was not a full-time service. I had considerable time to myself as well. Of course, I would have tried my best to help this person, without the promise of getting free art lessons, but to get art lessons from this artist was an opportunity I could not let pass. Briefly stated, I was able to help this person, and my art lessons began in short shrift. I kept up the lessons for a few weeks and then again, because of the press of the church duties, I had to drop them.

We lived in the house on 2920 26th Street for only four years and then moved to 608 34th Street. This new location was quieter and had fewer children in the block. It was also closer to the Pioneer church.

Chapter 23
SERVING CHURCHES IN THE RETIREMENT YEARS

As already indicated in the preceding chapter, the first church I served in retirement was the Pioneer Congregational United Church of Christ, 27000 L Street.

Pioneer Church is the oldest church in Sacramento, the present location being the third one. It has now a choice location and is equipped in every respect to take care of all of a thousand members. In fact, only about ten years ago, it did have over a thousand members.

Pioneer, by virtue of its history and of the membership of noted personalities in the past, has become a rather sophisticated church. In addition to having been a rather liberal church in the past, it also drew many liberal preachers. Pioneer wielded considerable influence in the past, locally, in the conferences, among other churches and in the community as a whole.

Pioneer was known to me since 1940, after my return from Argentina and the move to Lodi. Then and through the years, I was in contact with the Pioneer, its pastors and with the congregation. I noticed the changes developing in this church through the years, a change in the type of ministers, a change in the membership, and changing of objectives. The church usually had two to three ministers, as well as a minister of music and a minister of Christian education.

Within the last ten years, Pioneer went down in membership, so much so that it experienced an annual deficit financially and, in some years, it did not take up more than six members on confession. All manner of schemes and changes were initiated, such as changing time of services, orders of worship, outside speakers, cooperating with Episcopal Church, uniting both church school and youth work, beginning a Sunday evening celebration worship, largely for youth, but nothing seemed to bring back into the church the life and zeal a church should have. The attendance in the traditional service at eleven o'clock went down by the month.

First Congregational Church, Elk Grove, California.

What was the reason? I can only give my own evaluation, explaining the reason as I see it on the basis of many years in the ministry, in different countries and among English and German speaking people.

Most ministers, the last ten to fifteen years in Pioneer, seemed to think that Pioneer was still a theologically modern membership church. My eyes were opened when I began at Pioneer as pastor of Visitation and Counseling. Coming into the homes of people and talking and counseling with people, I heard the truth about the church, from the standpoint of its various members. The church now experienced the fact that it had changed its homogeneous nature to a heterogeneous membership. The strictly theologically modern membership of old is no more. Today, the membership of Pioneer has, by actual count: Old Congregational members, Baptist, Episcopalian, Presbyterian, Adventists, Church of God, Lutherans, Catholics, Mormons, and others. A church of this kind of membership cannot assume a doctrinal common denominator in the preacher's sermon and hope to succeed. The only workable common denominator a minister has in servicing such a church, or any other kind of church for that matter, is the Preaching of "The Word"—the preaching of the Gospel. And, this type of preaching was not very much in practice at Pioneer the last ten years or more.

It is my conviction that unless we return to the preaching of the Gospel, all churches will fail. Even now, it is a fact that the churches with the Gospel are succeeding.

THE CHURCH OF THE GOOD SHEPHERD,
Sacramento, California

My services at Pioneer Church lasted four and one half years. During these years, I had many occasions to preach in other churches on Sundays. One such church was also the above-named church, whose pastor after four years accepted a call from another church.

I enjoyed my work with Pioneer very much, but to work under another person with less practical experience in church work, and with a weak devotion to the Cause of Christ, was depriving me of the ability of doing maximum services at Pioneer. I knew what was good for the church, but my hands as part-time servant were tied. I had no freedom to be of maximum help to the church, hence I resigned and accepted a full-time service with The Church of the Good Shepherd, seven miles out of Sacramento, California. Good Shepherd Church was a comparatively new church in a new housing area and the members were upper-middle-class professional people. I was the third pastor the church had had so far. The church was organized in 1957 by the E.R. (Evangelical Reformed) and the first minister was of that denomination. My predecessor, just out of the seminary, took over and served the church for four years. This church was burdened with a heavy indebtedness at the time it affiliated with the Congregational church. This heavy property debt was a drawback in the church's growth.

The reason I took over this church was for its great potential in the area, and also for its strong young people's future. My predecessor, at the end of four years, gave up, saying his work was done.

Good Shepherd Church was a young church, not only in terms of the church building. The membership was young, with only about four families of retired people. Here, too, as at Pioneer, the membership represented many denominations and each member had his own ideas and voiced his wishes. I loved to preach in this church. They were so attentive and responsive. The youth work was a pleasure. I organized confirmation classes of twenty-five and twenty in the following two years. The young peoples' groups, meeting in the evening, numbered as many as thirty-five some Sunday nights. There was no end to making calls, but it paid off. In the time I was at the Good Shepherd Church, the membership doubled and many new activities were begun that united the church.

For a membership of about two hundred, the Good Shepherd church had a program commensurate to a church double its size. It was a friendly church and the people were not only willing to work, but able to work. If I should point out a weakness, it might be said that they were somewhat weak in their stewardship. The quality of giving has to be learned, and this church was on the way to experience the blessings of giving.

In the second year with the Good Shepherd church, I had to be hospitalized twice, because of a heart condition, staying in the hospital about ten days each time.

THE LOOMIS CONGREGATIONAL CHURCH,
Loomis, California

The second half of the last year in the Church of the Good Shepherd, I began to realize that I might need to take a smaller charge, as the work became too heavy for me. And so, at the end of a little over two years, I resigned, but with the following Sunday, the first of May, 1970, I began at the Loomis Church.

The conference office asked me if I would serve the Loomis church for a brief period, until they found a man to serve them full-time. I served the church Thursdays, Fridays, Saturdays and Sundays. They paid me three-hundred-dollars a month, which included car expenses. The distance from Sacramento to the church in Loomis was twenty-five miles, a fifty-mile daily trip and sometimes twice a day. Later in the year, the salary was increased.

The Loomis church is an old Congregational Church, organized in 1894. The buildings, church and parsonage, groaned under the many burdensome years. Some important people in the community had been active in this church in the past. Great choirs had been a blessing in this church in the past, and had been a blessing in this church through the years.

Still energetic in the work of the church, I felt with my years of experience, I could give this church "a lift."

The countryside of Loomis is so picturesque and the climate so wholesome, that I spent many hours in the country calling on people, on members and on prospective members. It was a fruit country and each farmer had his little orchard. Lately, however, with high cost of labor, the farmers had let their orchards dry up or uprooted them and sought employment in town with the government. Of the eight fruit sheds Loomis had, years ago, only two were still operating. The town of Loomis is still unincorporated, and it looks it, too. Age stares at you at every step you take in Loomis. In the outskirts, new houses are coming into view and, lately, more people from the cities are seeking the quiet and the beauty of the Loomis countryside.

The Loomis church had had many ministers in its time, ministers who worked hard and ministers who used the church mainly for personal advantage, and if these advantages were not forthcoming, they would move on or settle in the country.

The event that took place shortly before I took over the Loomis church is one that will remain unforgettable in the minds of the entire community, an experience that hurt the members of the church beyond recovery to its former position. It was no fault of the church, as such, or any of its individual members. It just happened to this church.

A rural church that once was able to maintain a full-time pastor was gone. To be able to have a pastor every Sunday, it had to unite with another church, or become a yoked church. Sometimes, a church would be able to have a minister who had another profession and preached only to supplement his income, or preached and on the side did some other kind of work to make ends meet.

Loomis had such a minister, well-educated, a good speaker, a former Baptist turned "modern," who supplied the Loomis church, but on the side traveled to many cities in the interest of fund-raising for churches. The result was that the pastor was unavailable most of the time, except Sundays. This was the beginning of the end. The main reason, however, for the tragic event in the history of the Loomis church, was the pastor's wife, who was also well-educated, but unsuited for a person in the parsonage. She was also a very sensitive person and had taken institutional treatments earlier. When the climate in the church became "stuffed," because of the pastor's absence, his type of preaching, and his leanings toward another denomination that negated the person of Christ, the church people began to think in terms of severing their relationship with him and informed him of this feeling in the church. When the pastor's wife heard of this, she became furious and wanted the pastor to do something. This produced a scene and she committed suicide in the sanctuary, near the chancel.

It was such a horrible tragedy, under such strange circumstances, and at a place least expected, that one is unwilling to talk about it. A pall was thrown over the whole community. We often speak of "the talk of the town," but in this case it was "the dark shadow of the town." To go to church and to be faced with the picture of this tragedy was too much for many and, as a result, church attendance reached the lowest level ever.

For a period of a few months, the church was served by visiting ministers and even lay people. With a handful of people in church and fewer than a dozen in Sunday school, the remaining faithful sorrowfully climbed the many steps to and from the church every Sunday, wondering what to do next. In the search for an interim pastor, the conference officials finally approached me to serve the church. I accepted, but only for a few months.

To assume a charge with such a background and with such limited possibilities, one faces the question, where to begin? To sympathize with the church, of course, is one of the first duties of the newly arrived pastor. But a church does not thrive on sympathy in the long run, and to do so would only demoralize the church. To succeed in Loomis, I did what I usually do when facing a counseling situation, where the counselee is as low as he can go. I find something in him that is of positive nature and then build upon it. So also it was with Loomis. I found many people with good qualities and still a firm belief that their church had a future. This was a good beginning.

In this church, as in many other old churches, there were elements of people who had become hopelessly set in terms of what would be good for the church. Changes giving the church new direction and offering it greater hopes for the future are seldom accepted. A case in point of this church was the need of a sidewalk and additional steps in front of the church. The rains had washed away the soil below the first step so it was difficult to take the first step up to the entrance of the church. Why was this situation tolerated for so many years? The architectural drawings for the remodeling of the front, including a sidewalk, were at hand, and the contractor, a friend of the church, was willing to give his time gratis to the church to have this job done. Why was the church so reluctant for so many years? In front of the church, many years before, six trees had been planted as a memorial to a family long ago passed to its reward. This was the reason. First, I tried to awaken the pride of the people in the church and to make the front of the church an inviting picture. Then, I sought out the two children, who now had families of their own, and talked to them about the trees. They soon realized that I was right and gave their permission to go ahead with the project of pulling out the memorial trees. As in former cases, so also here, I went ahead with the pledges, putting my name down first with one hundred dollars, and in a few days, we had the money to add two needed steps and pour the new sidewalk according to county specifications. This gave the church an inviting face. Someone remarked to me, "Pastor, you did what no one else was able to accomplish before."

Enjoying working with tools, I brought some along many times and fixed things up, both outside and inside the church. In the afternoon, as a rule, I made calls—many, many calls—first, on people who were members of the church but had dropped out because of what had happened. I made calls on present members who stayed at home, feeling ashamed and despondent over the event of the recent past. Gradually, the absent members, however, would show up and soon new ones would come. This was an encouragement to the few faithfuls. I taught the young adult Sunday school class, attended the ladies' organization regularly, helped with the new constitution of the church and made myself available for any other occasion when the church and community might need my services.

It all paid off. Old friends of the church became members and new people joined the church. At last the choir was reactivated and a children's choir was organized. The people began to smile again, which I thought was a good sign. An event of a different kind that gave the church a standing in the community was my participation in a panel in the school on "parent-teacher relationship." As a result of this public appearance and the remarks made there, the community was alerted to our church and its pastor. Soon after the panel participation in the school, I announced a class on "Family Life," to be held in the fellowship hall of our church every Wednesday morning from ten to twelve, open to any who might want to come. The result was very gratifying. As a result, many more new faces became familiar faces in the church.

Again and again, at the monthly business meetings, I let the pastoral committee report, but each time they came up with the same answer, "We are working on it." They simply were not in a hurry to have me quit. It was now over a year that I had served them. At the next business meeting, I said, "The last Sunday in June is my last Sunday with you." This did it, and the committee got busy. With the help of Dr. Norberg, the conference pastor, the committee finally came up with the name of a pastor that was accepted by the church and I left the church at the end of June.

Chapter 24
THE TRAVELING YEARS

Before writing about the four trips to Russia and other countries in Europe and Asia, it is very important to ask, "Why the emphasis on Russia?" There is a saying, "Where the cradle rests, one longs to be." In my case, there is so much not yet told, in terms of history, tragedies, sufferings and death at the hands of the government, that must be summed up and recorded, before I can write about the first trip to Russia to see what was left of my family.

In an earlier chapter, I wrote of the conditions in Russia when I left, and of my departure from Odessa.

The Russia Germans had, for years, planned in 1914 to celebrate the "one-hundred-fiftieth jubilee" in memory of the first settlers on the Volga. Elaborate plans were made to make 1914 the most memorable celebration in the history of the Russia German people. The reasons to celebrate were everywhere in evidence. The one hundred small mud-houses the twenty-seven thousand souls had occupied between 1764-1766 had grown to two hundred beautifully sprawling villages, most of which had a population of from ten to twenty thousand each. A wild country was now inhabited and modern culture was in evidence everywhere. But the celebration never took place.

At the harvest season of 1914, riders came by night, waking up the tired farmers from their sleep, and shouting, "War! War!" The weary farmers could not believe it. War with whom? War with Germany! Already by next morning all eligible young men had to be mustered in. Anyone not appearing was considered to be a traitor. Not a single one remained at home; all wanted to prove that they were loyal to the adopted country.

With the beginning of the war in 1914, the beginning of tribulation for the Russia German people came into every village. The speaking of the German language in the village was forbidden and all schools were in the Russian language only. The German men from the villages were told by the army superiors that they, too, were considered to be enemies of the country and woe unto him who was disobedient! He would be shot down on the spot!

But this was only the beginning of the suffering that awaited them. When in 1915 Germany had considerable success in the war against Russia, the German soldiers in the Russian army were blamed. As a result, no more German-speaking chaplains were accepted in the Russian army. In fact, all German-speaking soldiers were taken from the western front and sent into concentration camps in the Caucasus. There they were organized into work-battalions and treated as slaves. Doing some of the heaviest hard labor, they had insufficient food and water, and soon hunger-typhus broke out and took the lives of thousands. This was the case with only the soldiers. What happened to their families, and to all those remaining in the villages?

For several years already, a wave of propaganda had appeared in the newspapers, that the Russia German people were sympathizers with Germany and were under the direction of the German Reich. Even in the local newspapers, articles were printed by some of the highest officials against the German colonists. The German language was forbidden and anyone breaking the laws was sent to Siberia. What would happen next? Was there more to come?

Yes, more did come! In 1915, the government enacted a law to dispossess the German people of their land. The farmers had to liquidate their possessions in two weeks. Cows and horses had to be sold for whatever they would bring. All had to be gotten rid of. Some families had as many as six sons in service, but there was no exception made. No more land for the Russia Germans. There were cases of seventy-year-old parents who had six and seven sons in the Russian army, several of whom had already been killed in the war, who were sent to Siberia. The people were treated like criminals. The most prominent men in the villages were tortured and thrown into jails with the warning that if any agitation on their part should be created, they would be hanged or shot.

Who were the main spies and instigators of the persecution of the German colonists, who had sweated and with relentless hard work brought the land and their villages to model communities? These agitators were the Galicians, who observed the colonists with envy for their thrift and enterprise in the hopes of occupying their land themselves someday. These Galicians, breaking their loyalty to their own country, Austria, and fearing the arm of justice as the German army marched forward, received the land and the houses of the German colonists.

To Siberia! How many? Hundreds of thousands, like convicts under military cover and in convoys, were marched to Siberia, leaving behind their most precious possessions: fathers, husbands, brothers and mothers who, in the west, were giving their lives for the Russian country. The march was a long one, through cold and heat, snow and rain, hunger and thirst, to the land that even mentioning the name, Siberia, created an indescribable fear in their hearts. Many of these marchers to their new homes and villages in Siberia never reached the land. Even some of the strongest simply broke down and had to be buried in transit.

What heightened the tragedy of these unfortunate marchers to the east was that the sudden transport caused the separation of mothers from their children and husbands from their wives, some finding their family members many years later, but many never succeeding in finding their loved ones ever again.

Especially heartrending was the lot of those sent to Central Asia, largely due to the sudden change of climate to tropical heat, which these unfortunates could not stand. Thousands died as a result. With the intervention of the government here in Central Asia, it was made possible for these unfortunates to be sent back to European Russia, but only after half of the people had perished. They were quickly rushed to the railroad station and sent north to the area of Wjatka. Thousands of these unfortunates lived in barracks in the Orenburg area, a life all too often filled with tragic social consequences.

The story of the lot of most of the Russia Germans is so long and tragic that it would take books and books to do justice to the actual events and tragedies that took place in the years of World War I, primarily in the colonies from Wolhynien, Poland.

Before I can report of my first visit back to Russia to see my relatives, after forty-two years of absence, I must report the story of the revolution in 1917.

The Turning Point. The March revolution brought a change of government—Communism. The new government proclaimed freedom and human rights. But, this proclamation of freedom, in a subsequent phrase, did not pertain to the German colonists. Protests were lodged with the government by influential men, saying, this proclamation of freedom, by not pertaining to the German colonists, was casting a dark shadow upon the new government. The ice was broken when Kerensky informed the colonists that the reference to the "freedom" of the colonists was a misunderstanding.

The year 1918 seemed to cast its shadow far in advance. By October 1918, the Bolshevists had complete charge of the Russian people. Prisons were opened and many courts dismissed. The soldiers left the front and marched armed through the land. Latvian regiments offered themselves as personal guards and protectors of Lenin (Uljanow) and Trotzki (Bronstein). The Red Guard was composed of the darkest elements of people, who had no fear of any opposition. Millions of people, not only German-speaking, but of any nationality, were executed as the revolution took on momentum. Plundering, robbing, killing, destruction and raping took on the greatest momentum at this time.

In 1918, special attacks upon villages were organized, especially in the Volga. All monetary savings and agricultural products saved by the colonists were to be destroyed. All banks were nationalized. Whatever moneys and valuable papers the colonists had in their possession were taken from them. Two methods, "contributions" and "requisitions," were used to get the most out of the people. Through "contributions," the people were drained of their money and through "requisitions," the rest of their possessions were either taken away from them or destroyed.

A blooming German colony of over twenty thousand souls, Katharinenstadt, north of Saratow on the Volga, had been in the eyes of the Red Guards for a long time. One early morning at five o'clock, two hundred men, led by Czechs and Latvians with machine guns, marched into this great village. The church bells in the village were pulled to awaken the villagers. But it was too late to be prepared for the arrival of these bandits. Bullets were already flying upon those ringing the bells. All firearms had to be surrendered and the village rulers were arrested, as well as all other persons of influence in the village.

In the event of a missing father, another important member of the family was imprisoned. A state of war hung over the village. The village, now under military rule, was requested to deliver two million rubles under "contributions." Every day a new requisition was posted on the walls of the houses. Even the Red Guards knew that to deliver two million was an impossibility. But, the Red Guards were also willing to take less, as long as additional sums were regularly forthcoming. Having extracted all that the colonists possessed, these bandits finally moved out of the villages. What took place in terms of social behavior is impossible to describe. What happened in Katharinenstadt, happened in most other communities in Russia, from Siberia to the Black Sea. If the cash money was all extricated from the victims, new requisitions were imposed.

What happened in beautiful Katharinenstadt also happened in Schaffhausen, a colony of five thousand residents in early April of 1918. It was on a Sunday when the Red Guard fell into the village. The people were in church. A number of the Red Guard had been drinking before entering the colony and, in this condition, entered the church and in a few minutes the wildest scene took place. Women and girls were molested and, initiated by a number of young men of the village, a real fight began, ending in the flight of the Red Guard. Nineteen deaths were the final result of the Red Guard, but they also left behind fifty horses, twenty wagons, eighty guns, eighty pounds of shells and six hundred sacks that were supposed to be for delivery of grains. This was the first assault of the Red Guard in which they were defeated.

A fear of reprisals by the Red Guard left terror in the hearts of every person in the village. What had happened in Schaffhausen was brought to the attention of all neighboring villages and all felt they needed to arm themselves, and did so by obtaining all sorts of military equipment to be ready for the next assault. Those who were unable to obtain guns and swords took to the tools their forefathers had used in the fight against the Tartars: ax, fork, scythe and whatever else might serve as a good weapon.

As expected, the enemy did not waste any time in returning in a day or two, this time with a much greater number of men than the villagers could muster. The enemy did not enter the village, but fought at the edge of the village, losing with every attack. A new weapon was now used by the enemy. Three negotiators were sent to the village to offer conditions of peace. The two sides agreed on three points: first, the Germans would give flour and grain, free, in exchange for items the farmers had to buy in the nearby city of Wolsk; second, the Germans were to return all confiscated military equipment lost earlier; and third, a commission representing both sides was to meet to examine and ascertain causes and blame and to decide the nature of punishment of the guilty.

The German colonists, in all sincerity, met their obligation in full, only to realize that they had fallen into a trap. While the negotiations were taking place, the Russians gathered hundreds of men—factory workers, Austrian war prisoners, and ruffians of every type, to the new expedition to punish the colonists who had the nerve to challenge them.

On April 10, 1918, the not unexpected event took place. In groups, they moved into the village, into house after house, pillaging it of whatever they could lay their hands on. Whatever met them, they cut down. Women, children, the aged, all were killed. Many took to flight into the open country. Men would go after them and whoever was caught was murdered. Animals, too, were no exception. The best horses, cows and pigs were driven away by the enemy; other animals were butchered and loaded into the waiting wagons. All storehouses were emptied and plundered. What could the farmers do? They surrendered their weapons, and empty-handed, no resistance was possible.

What happened in Katharinenstadt and in Schaffhausen also happened to all the villages that came to the aid of the two above mentioned. All colonies lived in deadly fear of what might happen next. An unforgettable tragedy happened in Dobrinka, where children were raped to the point of death. In Warenburg, a bloody battle took place that took the lives of one hundred men of the village. They were tortured to death. Wormsbecher, who was to have been the leader of the uprising against the Bolsheviks, was, in the presence of the schoolchildren, his own wife and children, exposed, and hanged naked at the bell tower and left there for three days.

What happened in the Volga region also took place in the German colonies of Cherson, Taurien, Crimea and Bessarabia. In the Odessa region, my birthplace (Crimea), lived about two-hundred thousand German colonists. In 113 villages lived eighty-nine thousand Germans who owned four million hectares of land, fifty-eight percent of all the land in this region. Here, too, the German people had to fight to keep their women from being raped and their property from being stolen. In Odessa, like everywhere else where Communism had taken hold, the cruelest rule and killings of the opposition took place. The revenge on the German colonists reached its height in March of 1920 when thousands of colonists were executed. In all of the villages in the Odessa region, commissioners were assigned, who with the help of the Czechs, ruled the villages. Land and stock, all was socialized. As a result, acreage became limited and the supply of stock diminished radically. The greatest farmers of former years now had only about two horses (in 1921), and two cows. There was drastic need of everything, especially of clothing. People, especially children, walked in rags or went half-naked. The villages that suffered the most were: Lustdorf, Grossliebental, Neuburg, Marienburg, Guldendorf, Neulustdorf, Mannheim, Strassburg, Baden Salz, Rohrbach, Worms, Landay, and others. The end result for all the colonists in these villages was starvation of highest degree. Thousands starved to death in a region that was the bread-basket of the world during the Tsar years. During this crisis, the only hope of the people was to leave the country. But how? Some made it by night to Germany.

In the North-Caucasus, some of the most progressive colonies were found. Out of a wilderness, in ten years, forty villages with twelve hundred families developed a most colorful area of sixty thousand hectares of land. This area was cultivated, canalized and each colonist had the finest gardens around his place, kept green by several artesian wells. Most of these colonies were established and developed by Volga and Black Sea Germans. The inhabitants of this modern and up-to-date country had to leave what they had and in a few hours take wife and children and flee. Many of the other colonies in the area received the same order, to leave in a few hours. Where they would have to go or be taken no one knew, but they feared the worst. For most of these dispossessed, the only place to be taken was Siberia.

In later years, some had the opportunity to come back to where they lived before, only to find that either non-Germans were occupying their homes, or there was nothing to be found. The village was just bare land.

This was the case in Grossliebental, the village I described earlier, a modern village of rightfully proud people that, today, has but a few dilapidated dwellings occupied by strangers. I wanted to see this village on our trip to Russia, as indicated, but was not given permission to drive out there. My own nephews, who had been there the year before our visit to Odessa, reported that there was nothing left of the village, just ruins.

With the coming of Communism in Russia, as we all know, everything became nationalized. No more private ownership. Bolshevism now offered new slogans to follow that would bring well-being to all men. Peace, Land and Freedom—these were the solutions advanced by the Revolution. The masses welcomed these slogans and rejoiced over these new possessions. Peace, yes, all wanted peace, especially the soldiers, the millions of them, many of whom had spent three years in the war. "Peace now" was the slogan. "Stop the killing and the bloodshed, throw away your weapons, come out of the trenches and go home." This was the new Gospel of the Communists, and the average soldier welcomed this slogan. But, what a bloodshed followed—streams of blood, not against the enemy, but against their own brothers. Thousands were murdered, because of fear of those that might not accept this new slogan. Peace—what an empty slogan it was!

Everything was militarized, from the distribution of food to the distribution of factory labor. Everywhere the Red Guard was in evidence, and woe unto him who objected. Forced labor or death was the result. At the beginning, the Reds shouted themselves hoarse against forced military service, but now, woe unto him who did not volunteer for military service. Whoever did not volunteer was looked upon as a counter-revolutionary, and shot.

A condition of this nature produced many deserters, even at the risk of death, but all notwithstanding, the number of deserters increased from month to month. Entire deserter regiments were also convicted to permanent forced labor. Their relatives were arrested and all of their property confiscated. Conditions under the Communist regime had become may times worse than what the older family members had experienced under the Tsar.

One of the greatest blows our people had to suffer in the post-revolutionary days was the closing of the churches and teaching of their children in matters of religion. The Communists actually declared war on the Evangelical Lutheran Church, because they considered this church the church of the Germans. For 150 years, our people had adhered to and lived faithfully according to its teachings. Two thousand souls belonged to the Evangelical church and five thousand were Catholics. All this had changed—for how long? God only knew.

At this point, I want to come back to my own family in Russia. They, too, lived in villages and suffered like the rest of the colonists. My father, a leader in his village, never participated in the uprisings of the villagers, but could not escape the sufferings the villagers went through. At the time of the overthrow of the Tsar regime and the coming of Communism, when the colonists were deprived of all their possessions, and when everything became socialized to the point of suffering and destitution, the villagers where my family lived revolted against the Bolshevik government with the result that the Red Guard came to punish the revolters. Most of them had fled the village, however. My father, feeling he would be exonerated, not having participated in the revolt, remained in the village (Hoffnungsburg), loyal to his office as village mayor and head schoolteacher. When the Red Guard appeared, Father and two of my brothers were standing in the yard, wondering what might happen. They did not ask any questions, but simply gunned my father down. My mother subsequently sent me a leaf from a notebook through which the bullet had penetrated, as evidence of what happened to Father.

In the early twenties, many German-Americans received countless letters from their relatives in Russia, begging for food and packages. A famine caused by a drought had swept throughout Russia. Farmers left their farms for refugee camps where, in 1921-22, the American Relief Administration under Herbert Hoover at one time fed more than ten million daily. The famine, together with the epidemics in the refugee camps, took a toll of about five million people, who perished in the winter of 1921-22.

I had been in contact with my family intermittently. Sometimes, it took months before I received their letters, and then again, the letters sometimes would come faster. The reason for this irregular correspondence was that the relatives were not always sure whether or not it was safe to write. One day a letter came requesting me to stop writing altogether, stating it was unsafe to write and that all letters were censored, and considerable suspicion rested upon them because of their correspondence with me.

I never knew from month to month what might have taken place in my home in Russia. Patiently, I waited for them to write, before I would write again, resting uneasy for fear of the worst in my family. After waiting for three months for news from the family, a letter came. Mother wrote, saying, "It happened." My youngest brother, Paul, was banished to Siberia. What had happened was this: He was put in charge of requisitioning the grain from the farmers and was accused of not delivering as much as the government had demanded.

Soon after this famine, another one broke out, caused by the government itself by taking all the crops of the farmers in retaliation, because the farmers planted only enough for their own use, to forestall seizure of their surplus crops by the government, as was the case in the previous year.

I spoke of how my father was killed, how my youngest brother, Paul, was sent to Siberia, and now I want to relate the story of another brother, four years my junior, and what happened to him. I am relating this as I got it from my brother Edmund's wife, Emilie, who now lives with her son and daughter in Duisburg, Germany.

Edmund, my brother, four years younger than I, was imprisoned in Odessa because he pleaded with the authorities not to close their church. In Odessa, his wife, Emilie, went to see him weekly. She also did his laundry and, in his clothes, would put messages sewed into the seams. This was carried on for some months when, finally, she was told not to come anymore. He was transferred to Siberia. This was the last she heard of her husband.

While still living in Russia, in Lustdorf, near Odessa, at the time when Hitler ordered all Russia Germans back to Germany, where they were to become part of the Third Reich, the people were divided into groups; so many to a wagon and so many in a convoy. My nephew, son of Edmund, was a wagonmaster of one hundred wagons. One village, Grossliebental, alone, had eight hundred wagons. They started out on the trek to Germany on March 17, 1944 and were on the way three and one-half months. The German Wehrmacht would bring them food at times but, even so, they suffered untold hardships from hunger, cold and fear of attack and capture by the Russians. After they reached Yugoslavia, the men were taken into the German army and the women and children were sent to refugee camps, from where they were taken and placed on farms or anyplace where they could find work and have a roof over their heads. Thus, many families were separated until after the war. In the case of my brother's family, the youngest son, Paul, age fifteen, was lost and no word of his whereabouts found until months after the war was over, when his death certificate was located by the Red Cross, listing him as having died from the effects of war in a Berlin hospital. The oldest son, Waldemar, not knowing where his family was after the war, hoping that they would be reunited in their old home, asked to go back to Russia rather than stay in Germany, but instead of going to Odessa where all lived earlier, was sent to Novosibirsk, Siberia, where he now lives without any hope of ever seeing his family again. I will refer to him again later in connection with further visits to Russia, not long ago.

My sister, Ida, two years my junior, married to Alexander Floether, has met a similar fate, that of having been deprived of her husband one night and having been taken away, without any explanation as to why and where. To this day, she does not know for sure whether he is dead or alive or where he might be.

This is only a partial story of the vicissitudes my family went through.

Why was I spared all of the hardships my family went through? This question I have asked myself hundreds of times. I am not worthy of it nor ever will become worthy of this fortune, to be able to come to America.

The reader might remember what I said earlier about our departure from my relatives in Odessa, that my mother said, "I do not really know why you have to go to America." And, what she also wrote later, that she asked God, "Why?" and received the answer, "What I am doing now, you will not know, but will find out later on." When things became rough in Russia and thousands perished from hunger, my family had only one place to turn to, and that was to write to me for help. I had established myself in America, worked hard, advanced my education, finally became a minister of the gospel, and established a family of my own. I was able to send them package after package and hundreds of dollars to relieve their plight. One day, a happy letter from my mother reached me, in which she said, "Willie, now I know why you had to go to America. You saved our lives. Had it not been for you, we would have all starved to death." This was enough for me to feel that our God and Father had his hand in our lives. My guilt at having been spared all the hardships was now gone, knowing I was of some help to my faithful family.

Now, at last, I will be able to describe my first visit to Russia to see what was left of my family. That was in 1956. But, of my family, only the three oldest remained: Viktor, Ida and myself. Father was shot in the revolution, Mother died of sickness and my youngest sister died of typhus.

Many years had passed and I did not know the whereabouts of any of my relatives. When the wars had ended and the people so gradually found each other again, like my brother who was separated from his family for eight years, I began to plan to visit them. All of my remaining relatives—brother, sister, nieces and nephews—all live in Siberia. Knowing their addresses now, I proceeded to make plans to see them, should I be able to obtain a visa.

I had only one misgiving. Would it be safe for me to go back to Russia, having been born there? The misgiving was heightened when I applied for a visa to go to Russia. The visa was never forthcoming, with no answer ever given. Being determined in my desire to see my relatives again, I read in our church paper that a seminar of men and women was making a trip to Europe and to Russia. I applied to go along with the seminar and was accepted.

Again, I filled out the necessary papers for a visa and sent it to the Russian embassy in Washington. It was about a month before the departure from New York. In the meantime, I prepared for the trip, also inquiring about the status of former citizens of Russia, as I was, being able to visit Russia without encountering official problems. Among all the conflicting reports, one report came to me that others in the same condition as I was had been in Russia before. This strengthened in me the determination to go and my preparations to meet the departure date went along as scheduled. Day after day, however, I patiently waited for the visa from the Russian government. It was now time to leave for New York, but still no visa. In hope and trust that all my hopes would be realized,

I boarded the Greyhound bus to New York. Arriving in New York two days ahead of the departure date, I at once inquired at headquarters about the visa. "No visa yet," was the answer. The day of departure came and I was sitting on needles. Early in the morning on the day of departure, the telephone rang, and the voice of our leader, Dr. R. Gibbons, said, "Fred, your visa is here." In my life, I had learned to hope and to trust. It paid off here again!

One afternoon in June 1956, our plane flew in the direction of Russia. (Other countries in Europe were taken in first.) Our first encounter with the Russians came in Poland where we got off to dine and after that to go through customs. Even at dinner, the customs lady already began to assist the passenger ladies to declare their possessions, even their diamonds and wedding rings. As I saw this, anxiety again came over me. Before leaving and in preparing for this trip, I had purchased a dozen pairs of nylon hose for the womenfolk of my relatives in Russia, plus hundreds of dollars extra money for my relatives and three hundred dollars from my church members and friends to be given to their relatives in Russia. How would I fare, I thought to myself.

After the dinner, we were led into a large room with a long counter for the inspection of our luggage. I do not panic easily, but at this moment, I had to brace myself. One of the first pieces of luggage they opened belonged to the leader's wife. They went through it quite in depth and I thought mine would be next. Always clinging to hope in any situation and this was no exception either, I heard the customs officer say, "All OK." I could have shouted, "Yahoo!" for joy, but had to control myself.

The next stop was Moscow. I had agreed with my relatives beforehand to meet at the Hotel International. But, arriving at the hotel, I noticed my relatives were not there to meet me. I had no image of my relatives anymore. Forty years had passed, and with all the suffering they had gone through, the poverty and sickness that was so often part of their lives, they had changed so much. The two nieces I had never seen in my life. They were born after I left.

The fact, however, was that they were there in the hotel, but did not see us because we had been in the dining room. When I went to my room, I found a note in German, saying, "Uncle, we were here, but did not find you." I left the room, and as I went down the stairs, two young ladies were coming up the stairs. We passed each other, but then, each turning round and wondering, one of the nieces called, "Uncle!" That was it. We embraced and kissed each other and, in minutes, went downstairs and outside, where I met my brother Viktor and sister Ida. The joy was indescribable! After so many years, at last, to meet again! The questions to ask them were in the thousands, and the time to ask these questions was so brief. As per agreement, the trip included four hours a day sightseeing and part of that time I had to take in with the rest of the seminar members. I would, however, excuse myself for two hours each day to be with my relatives. We had, of course, the evenings to be with each other.

The uppermost questions in my mind were the questions about what had happened to the rest of the family in Russia. I was interested in details. There was much of the history of my relatives that was totally unknown to me. Even in subsequent visits to see my relatives, I was unable to gather the entire chronicles of my family.

My brother, Viktor, had gone through so much in his life, separated from his family for eight years, imprisoned, hospitalized for a long period of time, and hounded so much in his life by the Communists, that whenever he saw a police officer, he began to shake. In fact, one day in Moscow, while we were standing outside, he suddenly disappeared and did not show up until the following day. He said, "Whenever I see a police, I panic." For this reason, whenever we wanted to talk, we went outside, to the park or to someplace where we were alone.

The family members were poorly dressed. Their faces looked drawn and indicated lines of deprivation and suffering. They joined us for one meal at the request of Dr. Gibbons, our guide. The conversation between us was in the German language. My relatives spoke both German and Russian perfectly. They had a good education and were also holding good positions.

The days of our meeting and of questions and answers were only too few. Our time of departure for Finland came. The relatives saw us off at the station. It was a tearful parting.

This first visit with my relatives was just an opening of the reservoir of still unexplained family history, revealing just enough to make me become anxious to know what had happened next.

But, even for this brief visit, I was thankful beyond expression. They left for their homes in Siberia and we prepared to take the train to Finland. Before leaving for Finland, I cashed three hundred dollars in American Express Traveler's Checks, for rubles, some to give to my relatives and other money for relatives of my church members, who lived in the area my relatives did. (In Russia, you have to declare all the moneys you take into the country and when you leave, declare what you have left.)

The trip to Finland was an all-day train ride, not very eventful. The countryside became nicer as we came closer to Finland. Off and on we saw men and women in soldier uniforms, with rifles on their shoulders. As we were puffing and clanging along, the train finally slowed down and shortly came to a complete stop. A large gate over the tracks opened and slowly we drove into Finnish country. We all whopped it up for a while because we were now in a free country again. At no point during this first trip to Russia was there any problem about my citizenship. Later, I found out that after so many years out of the country, my Russian citizenship had become void.

Our trip to Finland began in Leningrad, where we had stopped for three days. Upon arriving in Leningrad, we were assigned our rooms and then went downstairs to look around and orient ourselves. Standing in front of the sidewalk, a lady member of our group came close to me and said, "Fred, don't look around, but you are being watched." Why? Of course, I watched myself, being careful not to do anything that would be against the law. I noticed that I was being shadowed by three officers. The only explanation I could give for this shadowing was the fact that I had cashed so many traveler's checks into rubles. Not finding me a dangerous character, they left me alone and we arrived in Helsinki safely and in late afternoon on a Sunday.

Even the air seemed cleaner and more exhilarating as we rode into the station of Helsinki. All of us seemed to sense an air of freedom in this beautiful city in Finland. The people were friendly and neatly dressed. Our hotel rooms were modern in every respect and the meals were superb.

I will not, in this chapter on travels, describe every country we saw. My purpose is only to emphasize the country of Russia and the meeting with my relatives.

The second trip abroad was by car and it did not include Russia. Mrs. Gross and I picked up a Mercedes Benz in Stuttgart and drove from there to Berlin, where we were met by another couple from the States, Mr. and Mrs. Bill Kuhrt, and together we toured many countries in Europe, seeing what we could not have been able to see without a car.

The next trip to Russia was in June of 1965. Mrs. Gross went along on this trip. We agreed in advance again to meet in Moscow in the Hotel International. In addition to meeting my brother and my sister with her two daughters, Helen and Emma, my nephew, Waldemar and his little girl, who lived in Novosibitsky, were all to be in Moscow. I had never met Waldemar, who was the son of my brother Edmund. We arrived in Moscow, expecting all to be there by the time of our arrival, but were disappointed at not seeing them. Viktor and Waldemar with his little Emilie had arrived, but no Ida with her two daughters, Helen and Emma. What had happened, we did not know, so I telephoned to Sarapul where they lived, to find out the cause of their failure to arrive. The answer was, Emma, the youngest daughter of my sister, had been taken critically ill, diagnosed as cancer, and they would not be able to come.

Having taken this long trip and gone through much expense to see my relatives, I tried to get permission, at any cost, to go to Sarapul by plane or train, whichever was possible. To get permission for this trip, I was sent to a number of Russian agencies and departments, but the answer was always the same—"Nyet." I called on the American embassy and also on the local American Express office to help me to get permission to go to Sarapul, but of no avail. Each time, the answer was, "Nyet."

With no further help available to visit my relatives in Sarapul, we made the best of the situation by visiting with my brother Viktor and Waldemar, my nephew, and his little daughter, Emilie.

My brother, two years my senior, has a wonderful memory and has a storehouse of information of the family history, but he was not very talkative. It was still too soon after the many ordeals they had gone through. Also, it was in my hotel room where we had gathered. When I asked him to talk and answer my questions, he answered, "Willie, these walls have ears." So, from then on, we would meet outside and, if possible, in the park, where we could talk freely. But even there, he never became talkative. In later visits, matters changed, as we shall see.

We made the best of the visit this time, taking in also many sights in Moscow, making purchases of special items to bring home with us and then got ready to fly down to Odessa, our birthplace. Viktor went to his home in Siberia, and Waldemar and his daughter went to his birthplace also, not far from Odessa.

A peculiar event took place when my brother left the hotel. Usually on these visits to Russia, we would bring gifts of clothing, shoes and other items. My brother had a sack into which he gathered his items. When we walked down the stairs and came to the bottom stairs, an officer approached him and asked him from what country he was. This, I could see, froze my brother then and there, and I quickly retorted in Russian, "Please, this is my brother." The officer sensed my sincerity and apologized profusely, and my brother and I went outside, where he took the taxi to the railway station. In subsequent correspondence, we found out all went well on his trip home.

Mrs. Gross and I took the flight to Odessa, where we planned to remain for three days. We looked forward to seeing Odessa, the place I had seen many times when I still lived in Russia. Odessa is a beautiful Black Sea port city. Many memories returned to me. About eighteen miles out was the once modern and beautiful village of Grossliebental, where my father and later my brother and also myself attended high school shortly before I left Russia for America. Many times, we would rent bicycles to pedal into Odessa and back. The road was excellent.

So Odessa had a strong attraction for me and I looked forward to seeing it. We occupied the Hotel Odessa, at the shore of the Black Sea, and had a wonderful view of the activities on the shore and the parading of people along the trottoir (promenade).

After lunch, we went to the office to arrange to go out to see Grossliebental, the village that was dear to us and the real reason we made the trip to Odessa. (In Russia, one can never transact business with the clerk or person who faces you; they are just contacts with the important people behind the scene.) We spent a few hours in the hotel office to obtain permission to take a trip to Grossliebental, but each time they had an excuse for not giving us the permission: the roads were bad, it was hard to get there because of recent rains, and even to arguing that there was no village by that name. Not getting anywhere, Mrs. Gross, in disgust, said, "You have no freedom here." For a while, I thought I might lose my wife! We really tried our utmost to see the village, but had to give up finally. As we stood there in disgust, they suggested we take in a meeting of the young people in a nearby historical building where a leader taught the youngsters to sing and told them of the heroes of the past and present. He was an energetic young man who, with the help of a few mothers, really succeeded in livening up the meeting. Besides us, there was also an Indian family and two sisters from New York present. We were requested to sit on the stage. The hall was filled to capacity, with about two hundred young people and some mothers, and with many inquisitive eyes directed upon us.

We had our interpreter along, who would put into English what we did not understand in Russian. The leader wanted each one of us to be introduced and give the name of the country we came from. After all had been introduced, the leader asked for one of us to give a brief talk. Not all stood up, in fact not any, so, being used to talking in public, I got up and briefly talked about family life, making use of the atmosphere of children and parents at the meeting. After the talk, a loud "bravo" sounded through the hall and I heard clapping of many hands. About a dozen youngsters came running up to me to kiss me. A girl came and pinned a red star on my coat. This, to a small degree, made up for the prior disappointments of not getting to see Grossliebental. It is also possible that with the happy reception of my talk, maybe my name received a plus mark in the Russian book of recorded names.

This trip from Russia took us to several other countries, first, however, by boat to Greece. I mention this trip to Greece only for the event, and the experience with a couple from East Berlin. It was a lovely trip to Greece. The people were all cheerful, at least they appeared that way. Toward the evening, a group of about fifteen were standing on deck, surrounding the captain, who was giving them instructions in case of an accident. After he had finished his talk, he left and the group continued on deck, talking casually, referring to their long train trip across Siberia and their different experiences on the train. I stood there listening, when one East Berliner asked me some political questions. I was frank in my answers, especially about Communism. I did not give Russia or Communism many compliments, especially after our recent experiences there. An attractive and intelligent young lady turned to me and said in German, "We like it in East Germany." By the tone of her voice and by her expression, I knew what she said was not what she felt. When the group dispersed, this young lady asked me for an appointment that evening, to which I agreed. At seven o'clock, she was at the door and knocked. For a solid hour, she related, quite in detail, all that they had gone through in East Germany. Yes, they got their education free, but afterwards, they had to give the state many hours of free services. "We are forever under heavy pressure by the state and have to keep account of all of our time," she said.

She was also a heavy smoker and liked good cigarettes but was unable to get any, even on board ship, because she lacked foreign money. I told her to come along down to the store, where I bought her two cartons of American cigarettes. If I ever saw a happy woman, it was this one! For months later, she corresponded with us.

The third trip to Russia was in June of 1966. Mrs. Gross was unable to go along this time and, in place of her, our eldest daughter, Grace Gammill, went with me. Because Grace had never been in Europe, we took in several different countries, beginning with France. Now again, as heretofore, the main objective was Russia. To make traveling for those in Russia somewhat less expensive, and for us to see other parts of Russia, we agreed to meet in Alma Ata, Kazakhstan. It was a five-hour nonstop jet flight from Moscow to Alma Ata.

When my daughter and I arrived, the relatives who were to be expected were all there, and stayed in the same hotel we did. It was a happy reunion between us and my brother Viktor, my sister, my niece and her two little girls, Olga and Lille, two pretty blue-eyed sisters.

Alma Ata has a population of about 500,000, and 130 miles from the Chinese border with the Tien Shan snow-capped mountains in the distance. The people were much friendlier here than in Moscow. Among the people, we found many Orientals and also a strong percentage of Mongols. The hotel was comfortable and the meals quite good. Our group always sat at a table alone. Even on crowded days, no one else was seated at our table. To our great surprise, the second day we found a tiny US flag on our table, something that never happened in Moscow.

As indicated earlier, a trip to Russia usually includes four hours of sight-seeing. Our guide was a young schoolteacher. As was always the case with our guides, the first day they eyed us with suspicion and anticipation; the second day, some tried to indoctrinate us; the third day, they became friendly and, if you stayed longer, the last day they shed tears when you left.

To show how differently we were treated here in comparison to Moscow, let me say that on every sight-seeing trip, we were allowed to take all of our relatives along with us free. The local official asked me each day if we were taken care of properly and if there was anything more he could do. In terms of friendliness and concern, this was a different country. One day, our sight-seeing took us out to a river-park area, a summer resort with many people. The river running through the area received its water from the nearby snow-capped mountains and was ice-cold. The people waded in the shallow parts, but could not stay in it for very long—it was too cold. Here we spent a few hours, talking with people and taking pictures. With a Polaroid camera with me, I took many pictures to the surprise of the onlookers, many of whom had never seen such a phenomenon. I had to prove it. My daughter, too, had a camera for slides and, together, we took pictures of all sorts.

When I began to put away my equipment, the guide came and whispered into my ear, saying, "There is an official here in the group who would like to have his picture taken." Through the interpreter, I asked him to pose. The picture was a real sharp exposure and he was delighted! Then the people around us wanted to have a picture of me, which my daughter took. I took my position, but in a minute, several others had gathered around me, even leaning against me for the picture. This picture, too, came out very well. Afterwards, one of the fellows beckoned me to come along. I asked my brother what he wanted. He said, "He wants to treat you with beer and vodka." He himself had had too much already. No, I did not follow him, but found a way out. It was a real happy sight-seeing trip, which all of us enjoyed. I could also see that my brother had regained his normal friendly face again.

One night, my daughter and I attended a Russian play. The attendance was excellent and the people seemed pleased with the performance. Next to my daughter sat a lady with her sister. During the intermission, I started to talk to this lady, in my halting Russian, and to my surprise found that she was a teacher of German in the Russian school. Thinking here was my chance to get the answer to the question I so often asked, "Why do we never get a chance to see an average Russian home?" I asked her that question. She was surprised and said, "Tomorrow at one o'clock, I will come over to your hotel and walk over with you to my home." I was very happy, because she was also a Russia German woman, originally from the Caucasus, earlier shipped to Siberia, as was the case with so many of the German people in the Odessa region and those of the Volga.

The next day in the forenoon, we again took in two hours of sight-seeing around town: libraries, tents of old tribal chiefs, a former three-story, all-frame structure, now a museum, and many other institutions. I expressed my pleasure over seeing so many wonderful things in Alma Ata. When we returned from the forenoon trip, the hotel proprietor told me, "There is a man here who wants to see you." Someone to see me? I had no idea I was known or had a friend here. The man who approached me said, in German, "I hear you are very pleased with our city and the sights you are seeing."

I said, "Yes, I am deeply impressed with everything we have seen so far." Then he asked me to talk over his radio station in the German language the following day at one o'clock, the hour of our appointment with the German teacher, an appointment I did not want to break. So, I had to turn him down. There are supposed to be ten thousand German-speaking people living in Alma Ata. They have their own German radio station, as well as a German newspaper.

In Alma Ata, we also visited a market; they call it a "bazaar." It took in several acres; a market where you could buy almost anything. I had frequented such markets many times when I was still living in Russia. This market, however, intrigued me. There seemed to be two classes of people selling and the produce seemed to be so different, one group cleaner than the other. With my relatives on hand, I began to ask questions. "Please," I said, "what is going on here? Why the difference, even in the expression of the people's faces?"

My brother looked at me and smilingly said, "My brother, here you have a picture of two enterprises, one a government enterprise and the other a free enterprise." In the free enterprise, the people grew their products independently, without outside labor. Thus they could sell whatever they had overproduced and the money made was theirs. They enjoyed it and were happy, which you could see here for yourself. The other was a government enterprise, and the clerks selling the produce cared very little how the sales went. In the meat market, the clerks wore white smocks, a sign they worked for the government.

I would never have been able to see such a market had it not been for my relatives. We all had a grand time. It brought many interesting memories back to me. How we loved to go to the bazaar in years past! And my relatives still frequent these markets regularly in their home towns.

Evenings, we sat together and went over unexplained family history. There were still so many unanswered questions about our past and about the circumstances under which members of our family had to give their lives. Viktor, Ida and I were the three oldest of the family of six children. So much of the family history had to be recorded and I was the least informed about what had happened in the past. At the same time, these special meetings gave all of us an opportunity to ask questions of each other's families as well.

The Alma Ata reunion was so far the best one. There was no danger, as far as we knew, of any spying on us, of any criticism, nor of any pressure brought upon us to do this or that. We felt freer here than at any place in Russia previously.

We had not met many Americans during our stay in Alma Ata. The second day there, however, a middle-aged man, clean-cut, stepped up to us and introduced himself as a *New York Times* reporter. He out-stayed us in Alma Ata. He seemed to know many people, who came to see him and with whom he had dinners. He was a pleasant man to talk to and occasionally ate with us.

The time to leave came again too soon, and saying goodbye to our loved ones was always hard on all of us. My relatives were four, with many packages added at Alma Ata. I had brought with me from the U.S. a large suitcase filled with clothing, used and new, many sweaters and many pairs of shoes. The suitcase was filled to bursting. I expected to have to pay duty on it in Moscow but, again, we did not ever have to open the extra suitcase. When leaving Alma Ata, we transferred all this extra weight to the relatives. In addition, they had items bought for their trip home. Altogether, they had twelve parcels.

They went downstairs with all their belongings and Viktor went in search of a taxi to take them to the railroad station. In the meantime, Grace, my daughter, and I went downstairs too, ready to leave. Our limousine was already waiting for us. Of course, we would not leave until my brother had come with a taxi. He came, but no taxi. By that time, the agent came, saw what was going on, and said to me, "Mr. Gross, what is the matter with you, why didn't you come to me for help?" He then ordered the limousine driver to go for a small bus, loaded up my relatives and took them to the station, gratis. We still had time to make the airport for our flight to Moscow later.

This was a good visit with the relatives in Alma Ata. Grace and I visited other countries also before flying home. On the trip to other countries, Grace and I compared experiences, to see which ones stood out as the most interesting and valuable ones. Grace referred to the Alma Ata experience at the river as the most exciting one. We went over it again, recalling the friendliness of the people. I referred to the visit in the home of the German teacher—how happily they welcomed us, served us, asked questions about the state of Michigan, where two of her brothers lived, and how we listened to her describe her work as a Russian schoolteacher. She lived in a very conservative home with small rooms, but apparently was satisfied because of the fair income.

Possibly the most exciting experience was the visit to the market, as described earlier and, especially, on the way back to the hotel on a streetcar, when a young man had a sackful of spinach with which he wanted to board the streetcar that was already more than full. The young woman conductor told him to stay off, but he insisted on getting on. When her patience gave out, she took the man's sack and, like a stone, just pitched it out of the car. Whatever she murmured to herself, I did not understand. I was glad I didn't. It was not complimentary, I am sure.

There were other incidents we recalled, laughing over some, and still getting annoyed over others. We recalled waiting at the airport in Moscow when the agent came, saying we had to pay for the additional weight of my hand baggage. Well, we got by. Grace recalled the incident in London when the agent wanted thirty dollars excess baggage payment for what we thought was an error on his part. With a hint from some American friends, we pulled ourselves out of that one too. There was no idle time on this trip. Excitement, all the way.

The last trip to Russia was in September of 1971. This was to be my last trip to the country where my cradle stood. We hesitated for a long time, because Mrs. Gross was not very well. The relatives in Russia begged us to come once more and make it a reunion in Moscow. Mrs. Gross and I went to our doctor and told him of our plans to go to about thirteen different countries, with the longest stay in Russia, and wished he might examine us and give us his reaction. Would he recommend our undertaking this rather strenuous trip? The doctor had been our family physician for years and had our histories in detail.

He examined us both at different times, gave us thorough examinations, made a number of tests, and then called us into his office, saying, "You may take this trip with confidence." We then went full speed ahead getting ready to go.

We were detained, however, not because of any cause of ours, but because of Mrs. Gross's sister, who was to go with us on this trip. She had some nurse's training, which would be a great help for all of us. Mrs. Caroline Hawley, Emilie's sister, came to this country as a child, six weeks old, and became a citizen through her father, as did my wife. Through the years in this country, she had taken her citizenship for granted and voted in all elections as an adult. She had never had a passport or been out of the country. This was her first trip abroad. When she applied for her passport, she was told that there was no record anywhere of her birth or when she had arrived in this country. Therefore, they could not issue her a passport. Here was a woman who came to this country at the age of six weeks, her father was a citizen of this country, she was now sixty-two years old, had six boys, who had all served in the U.S. army, and now she could not get a passport to travel abroad!

She tried everything without avail, and not even the local judge's word helped anything. She finally took up the matter with her senator in North Dakota and shortly thereafter her passport was forthcoming. The agreement was for her to meet us in Chicago, as our departure was from Sacramento, California. From this point on, all went well. In order to bring the latest information to the relatives in Russia, we stopped off at Frankfurt, Germany, to have a day's visit with my sister-in-law, Mrs. Emilie Gross, the wife of my brother Edmund. Her married daughter and her husband came to Frankfurt too. (My sister-in-law had never married again after losing her husband in Russia.) This reunion in Frankfurt was very important. My sister-in-law had a great deal of information about my family that we could not afford to miss. Her maiden name was Floether. She married a Gross and my sister, Ida, was married to a Floether, my sister-in-law's brother. Neither of the women married again after their husbands were taken away from them. So this visit with her in Frankfurt was very important to get all the available records of the family into proper perspective.

This Edmund family became divided, as was indicated in an earlier chapter, during the Russia-Hitler war in the forties, with Mrs. Edmund Gross and two children getting back to Germany and one son, Waldemar, remaining in Siberia. They never saw each other again. They corresponded with each other, but that was all. There was never any possibility of getting out of Russia, nor any permission even to visit back and forth. For one who has not gone through such an experience of losing a father, brother, son, and being divided, it is impossible to feel the pain of separation and the longing for a reunion.

The day spent in Frankfurt was only too short, but we had to meet our schedule. The next day we said good-bye, and our itinerary took us to many different countries, the main objective, again, Russia.

According to prior correspondence, the plan was to meet in Moscow, because the niece wanted her two daughters to become better acquainted with the capital of Russia. Another reason to meet in Moscow was the fact that, by now, the nephew, Waldemar, who lived in the heart of Siberia, had moved to Estland, closer to Moscow. The reunion this time, the last one, would not include sight-seeing. All five days in the capital city were to be for discussion and fellowship. In former trips, we always roomed in the Hotel International, but this time we chose the Metropol, an old but spacious hotel, with restaurants and coffee nooks on different floors.

Our arrival was delayed by a downpour of rain that later turned into snow. This delay prevented our landing in a larger airport. Circling for some time, the signal to land was finally given. It took us two hours to get through customs, mobs of passengers causing a congestion, the kind I have never seen in Moscow. Declarations had to be filled out in either Russian, English or German. The people were frantic in search of a form they could understand. Passengers were directed to one passage way, then an official came and directed them to another gate. This was one time the Russians were poor masters of the situation. Children cried, little fellows lost their parents, and others could not find the rest rooms, a confusion I had not seen anywhere for a long time. Had the officials insisted on going through our baggage, we would still be in the airport waiting for clearance.

It was a ghastly drive from the airport by taxi to the Hotel Metropol: rain, snow, poor visibility and slushy roads, but we finally made it safely. At the hotel, we were directed to our rooms and, in a short time, all was forgotten in welcome sleep.

The anxious moment and the concern the next morning was, "Are they here? Are all of them here?"

I went downstairs to look around, but saw no familiar faces anywhere. I went out on the sidewalk and looked there for a familiar face among mobs of people, on foot, by bus and by taxi, hither and yon, going to work and to destinies known only to them. I went inside again and finally stopped at the main entrance of the hotel, keeping an eye open for a familiar face. Someone touched me from behind. "Hello, uncle," said the voice—yes a familiar voice. It was Helen, my niece. "Where are the rest?" I asked. "Uncle Viktor and Mother are out at the edge of town, the only place where we could find room. Uncle is getting very discouraged, wondering whether or not you were coming."

We took a taxi and in less than an hour we arrived where they roomed. Helen and I walked toward the room. The door was slightly open and there was Viktor, who burst out and said,

"Willy, you are here!" Both Viktor and my sister Ida greeted me with a feeling only we can understand. They had been walking the floor, suitcases still packed, awaiting my arrival, really Helen's, because they did not expect me to drop in just like that. We quickly loaded their items and drove back to the Metropol, where all the rest waited in our room, all except Waldemar. The joy was great!

Before we had time to sit down, Helen, my niece, said, "Let us first of all pray." She began first, then several others, prayers of thanksgiving, filled with emotion, for this historic and possibly final reunion of people who had gone through hair-raising experiences in the many years past.

The first duty of the moment was for the relatives to get their rooms assigned to them. This was just a matter of form, because the rooms were procured before and were already paid for. We tentatively agreed on the plans for the five days of our stay at the Metropol. The hotel was immense. It was necessary to orient ourselves first to know where the restaurants were, the stores and the various offices.

Waldemar, now living in Estland, arrived a day later. Since we all wanted to be in the same hotel, he and I went down to the office to get his room assigned and get him registered. It took us an hour to get one room. The ladies at the desk, very courteous and proficient in the English language, waited on us. As I indicated before, the clerks one faces do not have the final word to say. The telephone connecting the clerks with the men behind the screens is always hot. They first tried to refuse me the room where we were lodged. In the vouchers I had with me, one was for a room for my nephew and that was my strong point. After much harassment, discussion, explaining and hee-hawing, I was granted a room for my nephew. The two ladies waiting on us were just as happy as we were. I paid for the room with the voucher and then we were sent to the room clerk, who, after looking at the passport of my nephew, gave us the room number. What an ordeal! Later, to show my appreciation to the two ladies for their patience and perseverance in obtaining the room for my nephew, I bought a nice bouquet of flowers and some chocolates, which they accepted graciously.

From now on, we felt at ease, having all the business part of this trip transacted. Now we needed to get acquainted with the restaurants, the coffee shops and the different stores.

The main restaurant was on the first floor, an immense area, divided into two sections, the breakfast-lunch area and the dinner area. The table setting, linen, and table-ware were ample. As you entered the restaurant, you were pretty much on your own to find a place, and the hostess was very rarely seen. With all of us having meal tickets, we could eat individually and in groups. We tried at least once a day to eat in a group. There were nine of us and for all of us to eat at the same time, at the same place, was a chore. But, one meal a day, we managed together. The menus always seemed to be scarce, one to a table, no matter how many were at the table.

The meals were fair most of the days, but lacked vegetables and fruit. The noted borscht is no longer what it used to be. It now is adulterated and has lost its seasoning and ingredients that made it a delicacy, both in taste and smell. There was always plenty of liquid refreshment, and two kinds of caviar in abundance. The service and the attitude were far from an inducement to eat. Somehow, the clerks and waiters everywhere give you the impression that the important person is not the customer, but the person who waits on you. The clerks sit and chat with one another, and will ask you what you want only when they are good and ready.

At the small eating places within the hotel, and where we paid for the meal in non-rubles, the service was better and the waiters seemed to reflect an occasional smile. Possibly it was because tipping here was quite in practice. One could order better food, too.

The stores in Russia, and notably in Moscow, are of three different kinds. First, the regular store, where you may buy almost anything you need and desire, but not of good quality. A second kind is where you can buy better goods, not found in the regular store, but before you can buy there, you must secure a certificate from the bank which takes a few days to obtain. In the meantime, you are investigated as to where you have gotten the money from to buy better goods. What a control Russia has over its people!

The third type of store is called Beryoska, where you cannot buy with rubles, only with dollars, pounds and a few other foreign moneys. In these stores, you can buy really wonderful things, even American cigarettes at less cost than in the States.

The Beryoska in the Metropol hotel was well patronized and by us as well. A Belgian stood before the Russian jewelry counter and, with beaming eye, had picked an item for his wife, but when he came to pay for it, the clerk said, "Nyet!" He had handed her Belgian money, which was unacceptable. He looked sad and turned to me and said, "Could you help me, please? I will give you rubles for dollars." Feeling sorry for the poor man who wanted to buy his wife a precious homecoming gift, I exchanged twenty-five dollars for rubles for him. He was so happy that he kissed the hand of Mrs. Gross and her sister, Carrie.

On the day before leaving Russia, we spent a couple of hours in the Beryoska, going through many items that we Americans wanted, and finding what we wanted to buy for the relatives. The relatives, too, had many items that they wanted and needed desperately for themselves. My brother came to me with the special question, "Could we get the money that you said we were getting from you, in dollars instead of in rubles?" It did not make any difference to me at all. They knew this from the night before, when we had talked about their transportation costs, which I always paid, when coming to see them. And this trip was no exception. The transportation paid for, and for brother and sister a few hundred dollars extra, enabled them to buy a good many items they had needed for a long time, as well as items they could not buy at all without dollars. It was a great day for them and this was reflected on their faces. Even the clerks threw an envious glance at their countrymen buying with dollars some of the most luxurious items which they, the clerks, could never afford to buy.

On the last evening in Russia together, we had another important discussion, questions and answers, as well as comments on a variety of subjects. What had been on my mind for many years was the matter of the standing of the Russia German people in the eyes of the Russians now. During and after the war periods, the Germans were looked upon as traitors and enemies within the country. How was the feeling now? It was my nephew who spoke up first. He was a highly skilled electrician and well-versed, both in Russian and German. He said, "Today the feeling is reversed. We are no longer being hounded. On the contrary, we are being sought out and we never get jobs others dislike. We are respected by the officials." The logical question was, why? This reversal of attitude toward my people in Russia must have a good reason. Deep down in my heart, I knew the reason, and have known it for many years, but I was anxious to have it made audible by this young skilled electrician. He said, "The Russian officials and leaders have again found out that the Russia Germans are hard workers, are dependable and do not waste time on the job. They are naturally skillful and able to do many things. In the past," he said, "we were shunned. Today we are being sought out."

I must say I found that out already on the previous visit in Alma Ata, where ten thousand Russia Germans live. They revolutionized that country, making out of it, as in the Ukraine and on the Volga, a paradise out of a desert. This was the case with our Russia German people wherever I found them, in Canada, in Argentina, in Brazil, and in the United States. Everywhere, they proved themselves hardy, industrious and faithful workers and citizens. And so, to hear it again in Russia from a fourth-generation member, was glory enough for me. The true character of the Russia German people still lives wherever they are in this wide world.

The other matter we discussed was religion. One hears so much these days about religion in Russia, reports that very often are in conflict. In every visit to Russia, I was able to visit churches, both Catholic and Protestant, the cathedral and the big Baptist church. In both cases, the attendance was far above what I had expected. Twice in previous times, the attendance at the Baptist church service was two thousand, the service lasting for two hours. Rarely had I seen such interest in church as here. In the cathedral, too, I found both young and old present, coming and going, participating in the rituals of their church.

All of this notwithstanding, the criticism of the church persists. The number of churches is restricted to so many churches for so many people. I saw many active churches being refurbished to look attractive inside and out. There was only one small church I felt like picking up a brush and going to work on. There are even new churches being built. A Lutheran church of three hundred seating capacity was recently constructed.

The persistent criticism of the church is often made by people who have an ax to grind or who have ulterior motives in mind. Bringing up this subject of religion in our group discussion and talking about the present status of religion, we wondered why criticism of Russia about religion seems to continue endlessly. My niece, a married woman with two children, whose husband has a good job and who has a good job herself, finally spoke up. She said, "There are two types of Baptist churches in Russia." (The Baptist church was always the strongest Protestant church in Russia through the years.) "The one type of Baptist church in Russia has an open membership; that is, the government has access to the list of its members. The other type of Baptists say it is not the business of the government to know who the members of our church are. Since they do not divulge their membership list, they are the ones being persecuted. The government insists, however, upon seeing the list of church members. For this reason, the latter type Baptist church has gone underground and is still being persecuted in Russia."

There are many Russians returning to the church. Even some party-members have their children christened. Christianity in Russia is not dead. In fact, I look to Russia to see there one of the greatest revivals of religion to take place in the not-too-distant future.

The day of departure came and all of us were sad. This had been a wonderful reunion in every respect. For five days, we visited and exchanged thoughts, talking about the great problems of life, of what the future might have in store for us, and now, again, the time to say good-bye was here. The mixed feelings about the destiny of man comes to the fore in moments of this sort. What has the Almighty in mind for us? What is the Mission of a people, as God sees it? What lessons do all these hardships and privations, persecutions and death, have to teach us?

Who has the answers? Only God! But, what about us, His creatures? What are we to do? How are we to go on in life in order to prevail? What is there that will sustain us in the hour for which we may not be prepared? I can speak only for myself. And, what I have tried to do through the years of my life, in good as well as in ill days, was simply to keep the faith. Without a faith, a trust, life has no meaning. Clinging to the faith, many questions as those raised above, will, in time, bring an answer. Hundreds of times I have thought of what my mother said, praying to God, asking why her son had to go to America and, receiving the answer, "What I am doing now, you do not know, but will find out later." The answer came, "You saved our lives, we would have starved to death." Time and faith are two ingredients that will never let you down. They have been my stay through the many years of my life, years many of which were really rough and taxed my very substance. Faith and time (call it patience) steel a man to action and final victory over any trial.

These discussions on our last evening together were also hours of deep reflection over the way the Almighty has led this family of ours. Our questions may not all have been answered, but one thing is sure; we have greatly profited by these vicissitudes.

With prayers and well wishes, our historical meeting came to an end. In a few days, we were home again.

Chapter 25
SOME THOUGHTS ON COUNSELING
Background and Process

My interest in counseling goes back to the study of psychology in the University of North Dakota at Grand Forks, North Dakota, and to the fact of my chronic lumbago that plagued me for many years.

This chronic lumbago had plagued me intermittently for more than ten years. I sought help from many doctors, but never found any relief. One doctor in the Quain and Ramstadt Clinic in Bismarck, North Dakota, examined me and frankly told me that there would not be any relief and that I would have to bear the ailment the rest of my life. To provide relief, he prescribed for me a wide belt made of soft leather. With this discouraging advice, I went my way and carried on my ministry under great difficulty, sometimes with excruciating pain and with many discouraging moments.

Secretly, I did not take the doctor's diagnosis as final. In fact, from that moment on, I planned and prayed that the all-wise Doctor would have relief for me some time in the future. My faith in recovery had never weakened. It was only a matter of time when relief and eventual cure would come. The leather belt in the meantime was used by me, as well as by many of my parishioners with the same affliction.

My interest in psychology, as indicated, increased by private study and later by more formal education.

Even though I was afflicted with this periodic lumbago, I nevertheless made the move to accept the commission as missionary to Argentina, still hoping and praying that recovery would return to me. In Argentina, I continued having periodic attacks of lumbago. Again, I would consult local doctors, Argentine, Swiss and another American doctor, who spent half a year in Argentina and half a year practicing in America. The doctor's examinations were very thorough, even to making blood tests, but they never made any suggestions, and no help came.

My work in Argentina and Brazil necessitated traveling by rail, bus, truck, ox-cart, on horseback and on foot. I would also carry with me two suitcases, not only of clothing, but also of books. This load was a strain on my back many times. Only he who has had a similar experience will appreciate the excruciating pains one has to suffer. I carried on without taking time out to nurse my pains.

On one of my long trips north to Formosa and the Chaco, I first called on my family in Buenos Aires, where the children went to school. The day before leaving for points north, I went to a German library and, perusing through the books there, I came across a German booklet entitled, "Suggestion und Hypnose" (in English, Suggestion and Hypnotism). The title of this booklet struck me and I bought it. This booklet became my reading on the trip. Not only suggestion, but also autosuggestion, was treated in detail. It also gave detailed methods of treating many ailments by autosuggestion. The emphasis was on how experiences would settle in one's subconscious mind. I read the booklet through twice at one sitting and later again and again, until I became thoroughly familiar with its content and the principles of curing ailments by autosuggestion. I began to feel relief on the second day. The process of suggestion and autosuggestion was from then on a daily practice in my life. Two weeks after reading this booklet, I found myself a cured person and have been ever since. No more pains, no more standing on one leg when preaching. Before, I could hardly tie my shoes, or work in the garden for more than five minutes. Now, I can work like a horse. My true self came back again. What a relief! It paid off to have faith and to wait with time.

There is a biblical reference which says, in essence, "Whatever happens to you, let it serve you to the best." I accepted this as a principle to go by and to apply it in my life. It paid off. As a result, I became not only a healthier person, but also a better counselor. I could talk of experience, which is always a good teacher.

Through the years in my counseling, I would keep in mind that a person should never give up. I was able to suggest to people in distress never to resort to drastic measures to solve their problems. If a person is "low," there is only one way to go and that is up. There is never a person so devoid of a quality that he is not worthy of rescue. To build upon a good quality, however small, is the greatest challenge of any counselor.

There are many counselors practicing the art today. Some are counselors because they have had a hard time becoming a success in the occupation they are in. For them, counseling is a way out. Such a counselor will never succeed. Others are counselors because of an acquired knowledge of the subject and feel the urge to put that knowledge into practice. It is important to know the process of counseling, to apply the many methods of counseling, and to have a large store of knowledge of psychology and psychiatry. To read all the available books on counseling is imperative, if one is to succeed in counseling. But, all of this is not enough.

The true counselor, successful in meeting and understanding people, has to be born with the correct mental and emotional equipment. Having that, education and a store of knowledge are an additional help to becoming successful in this field.

To be able to establish rapport or the state of empathy was never hard for me. And, once you have that relationship established, the process is relatively easy. Some use the directive method, others use the non-directive method. I use both methods, depending upon the individual. Some counselors are introverts, others are extroverts. Each needs to be treated differently. There is always a way of treating a person, and the counselor has to find the way to treat him.

In the case of children, I often used play-therapy and role-playing. Watching the way children play, with what they play and with whom they play, is quite revealing. An example of a ten-year-old girl might be of help in understanding what I mean. This girl was playing with the toys in my counseling room. On the floor, I had a rag-doll family; father, mother, a brother and a sister, all in a row. Looking at me first, the girl then walked over to the rag-doll family and stepped upon the father. This was, to me, indicative of what her trouble was. I, from then on, counseled with the parents and found that there was a poor father-daughter relationship.

Not infrequently I employed dream and nightmare interpretation. The subconscious is honest. In the subconscious we are the stage, the actor and the manuscript. We dream of that with which we are concerned in life. An important example came to my attention a few years ago. An eleven-year-old girl had nightmares every night at ten o'clock. The parents took her to two psychiatrists, each one giving a different interpretation of the girl's problem. Upon the suggestion of my wife, a schoolteacher, the girl came to me. The problem was that the child would not tell her mother, nor her teacher, what she envisaged in her nightmares. How was I to go about finding this important information in order to arrive at a possible solution of this case? I thought of resorting to role-playing. I had two toy telephones in my room. I gave the child one, and I used the other telephone. We began to converse, she assuming the role of her mother and I the role of her grandmother. We talked as mother and grandmother would ordinarily talk, when all at once, I asked, "Oh, by the way, does your girl still have nightmares?" She said, "Yes." Then, in a few minutes, she told me all she saw in her nightmares. Thus, I determined that there was a conflict between her and her twin brother, who was taken every place, but she was left at home. I began to counsel then with the father, who was happy to make amends by taking her along with the twin brother, resulting in the cessation of the nightmares.

Dream interpretation worked with adults as well. Knowing the symbols of dreams, I was able to interpret many, if not most, of the dreams.

An example was of an adult, married, with one child, who was plagued by a nightly dream that he was killing his father (who really was dead). and he became so obsessed with this dream that he confessed to his wife he felt the urge of killing both her and their child. His wife came to me first to relate their plight. I suggested that her husband come to me if he was willing and we would all three cooperate in solving the problem. He came and talked quite freely, hoping to become a normal man again. I asked him about the size of the family. He said, "We have just one child, who was adopted." This fact gave me the first clue to the problem and the solution from then on became quite easy. Knowing the symbols of dreams, I could explain to him what he was doing subconsciously. Their child was an adopted child because the husband was unable to father any children. He was examined by four doctors and each one had the same diagnosis. The wife wanted to have a child, but how? She suggested artificial insemination, to which he violently objected. They then agreed upon the adoption of a child. They both loved the child and she was a sweet and, in every respect, a normal child. But, this man was subconsciously brooding, because he was killing his manhood (gun and father-manhood).

In looking over the many cases that came to my attention, I found that most problems with which people were afflicted, were the cases of children, conflicts in the family, parent-child relationship, sibling problems and unloved children. In the case of adults, most cases had to do with husband-wife relationships, incompatibility between the spouses, triangle cases, deep-seated anxiety and lack of love.

My counseling years were happy years and still are. Even though I am retired, my counseling goes on, less frequently, however. Living in the area between Stockton and Sacramento, many people have become known to me, and I to them, which brings us together, especially when problems arise.

To be both counselor and pastor is a distinct advantage. Not infrequently the problem has to do with religion, especially when the counselee has a religious background. An example was a young man of high-school age who was troubled after hearing a "fire and brimstone" sermon. So plagued was he with guilt feelings that he wanted to end his life. His parents took him to a psychiatrist, an acquaintance of mine, who called me up, asking me to counsel with this young man. With my religious training, and being familiar with the different teachings of churches, I was in a good position to help him to help himself.

Another case was of a well-to-do woman, quite intelligent, who, after consulting with both a psychologist and a psychiatrist, came to me for help. She eyed me very carefully and proceeded very cautiously to relate her problem. It took weeks of long sessions. She was plagued by deep-seated guilt feelings of what she had done in her high-school years. As a final resort, I suggested to her the only next move for her to follow, as I saw it, was for us to go down on our knees and have her ask God for forgiveness. She really was in earnest now. I prayed also, asking God to be merciful unto her. She went home and, in a few days, called me up, saying, "All is well now, I have peace in my heart."

It is a rewarding feeling when people come back to tell you how much the counseling has helped them. Sometimes counselees would write to express appreciation for help received.

Aside from the people helped directly, there have been several cases where people in the community expressed their appreciation for the help that came to the community through the counseling services. One such letter came from a person I never expected to be much interested in what I was doing as pastor and as a counselor. Here is the letter:

Dear Reverend Gross,

You may perhaps be surprised to receive a letter from one not of your congregation, but we want you to know that there are others in our community who have enjoyed your presence among us and will miss you when you leave.

We appreciated so very much your work in the saving of one marriage that was brought to your attention. No one can estimate the ultimate value of such a service, as it affects the lives of so many besides the two principals.

This is just one instance that we happened to know about, and I know there are countless others.

Elk Grove is a better place for your having been here.

This old world could use more people like you.

Harry and I wish you a pleasant retirement with only peace and happiness and good things coming your way.

Sincerely yours,
Florence Markhofer.

More and more ministers are studying the art and process of counseling and rightfully so, because of the constant need to be of help to people, not only people in your parish, but because of the need in the whole community. The pastor is a necessity in every community.

In taking counseling in the University of the Pacific, under a psychiatrist, Dr. Scheuerman, the question was asked one night by a student about the value of a pastor in counseling. Unhesitatingly, he said, "A minister is worth more than five psychiatrists." I was very happy to hear this statement.

Chapter 26
SOME THOUGHTS ON THE CHURCH AND THE MINISTRY

With fifty years in the ministry in this country, in Canada, in Argentina and Brazil, in the German and English languages, getting involved also with racial groups, I can conscientiously say that there is no profession that can be compared with the call into the ministry, especially if the ministry is coupled with the art of counseling. There are many professions in which, if one is conscientious and thorough, one can be of real service to humanity.

The ministry, however, is primarily one of service to the people's spiritual needs. For that reason, the ministry of the Gospel is unique. The ministry, therefore, has the potential of rendering a supreme service to mankind.

The "calling into the ministry" is usually connected with the church, an institution brought into being by Christ himself. The church is, therefore, not like any other organization, club, lodge or sorority. The church is of divine origin, based on the faith that Jesus is the foundation of the church with the promise that it will never fail. It will suffer, have its high points and times when it will be persecuted and diminish in its membership, but it will not perish from the earth. The church's program is always the same—to save people and to make known unto them the Love of God and in His name to go to the ends of the earth to proclaim the will of God.

The church consists of people of all nations, regardless of color, tongue or status. The love of God does not recognize diversity. It is a community of kindred minds.

The existing denominationalism through the years will possibly continue to be with us in the years to come; it is not the essence of religion. The division of the church is due to many reasons, but never because of the love of God. Love of God and service to man are the same in any language, in any country and the same with rich and poor. Christianity is, therefore, a universal religion.

Denominationalism is of man's origin. God does not will it. It can be frankly said that denominationalism has lost its emphasis, and will, in the future, be less and less practiced. The last twenty-five years have brought many denominations together, if not into organic union, then at least into closer cooperation with each other. How I remember those years when, apparently sincere, although misguided, people would say, "Unless you belong to my denomination, you will not be saved." Those days are gone, hopefully forever. The trend today is to unite and, if at all possible, to unite organically. It is a slow process, but a process it is, to unite.

There is a strong current today to disassociate oneself completely from the church, because of its many mistakes and its disinterest in the problems of society. The criticism may have an element of truth, but that element of truth should not become the reason to disassociate oneself from the church.

Man is a social animal. He does not live by himself; he seeks fellowship and does so all around us. Whenever two or more people of similar minds find each other, they will eventually begin an organization. And the organizations that we have are legion. Christianity is no exception. By its very nature, Christianity seeks other Christians and, sooner or later, a church is founded. I have found this especially to be true in my missionary years in Argentina and Brazil. As soon as the farmers in frontier countries established themselves and became rooted in the new areas, they would build a church to meet for fellowship. At times, they lived in utter poverty and deprivation, but together, they would come to worship God. Many times they had modest church buildings of clay and seats of boxes, some even sitting on the floor, but they had a church. What Jesus said—"Where two or three come together in my name, I am there"—I found to be true again and again.

The church will always be with us, to the ends of the earth. Denominations change and become lesser in emphasis, but the Love of God and the Spirit of Christ will never change. As Christ has said, "I am the same, yesterday, today and forever."

We need this faith in God and Christ more than ever before. And to be able to hold this faith in God, we need witnesses to that fact.

As soon as the church was established, the members appointed men and women to carry on the cause of Christ; preachers, missionaries, teachers and social workers.

How important are the ministers? How do they become ministers? What is their motivation? What were the ministers like in the past? What does the new "breed" of minister look like and how does he operate? These are all important questions. I may not attempt to answer them all, but, nevertheless, I must record my reaction to the conduct of many of the ministers of today.

The church pastor comes from the church, is a member of the church, and is dedicated to the church as the servant of God. He is the shepherd (pastor) of the church and the servant of God. He exists and serves because of the church. The church was first, then came the pastor, ministering and shepherding the church.

From the beginning of the church and through the years, before the minister assumed his duties, a more or less elaborate service of ordination took place, consisting of brief talks, praying and laying on of hands, thus making the candidate for the ministry feel the importance and the sanctity of his calling.

With my German background, leaving the old country at the age of eighteen, I can very vividly remember the attitude of our people toward the pastor. He was looked up to as a man called by God, to devote his whole life to the shepherding of his flock, caring for their spiritual needs and laying down his life for them. The pastor was honored, not so much for his person, but for the cause for which he dedicated himself. The cause, of course, was the Cause of Christ. And, in our eyes, as young people, we always felt that there was no greater cause than to answer the "call," if and when it came to you. The pastor of a church, in my memory in the old country, stayed, as a rule, for many years, if not his whole life, in one church. This was largely due to the conception of the people about the ministry.

Another important function of the pastor in the early churches was that the minister was primarily the servant of God, to preach "The Word," the Word of God, and secondarily perform all the other functions that a pastor was asked to perform.

Looking back over the years and including the years in America, I have found that the later ministers and especially so many in contemporary times, have deviated drastically from preaching the

Word of God. To raise the question, Why? would possibly take a book to explain. Here, I want to give just a few reasons as it appears to me, why so many ministers do not preach the Word of God and prefer to preach on contemporary problems and social issues.

I would like to point out two factors in the life of the later ministers that, as I see it, have brought so many churches to regress instead of progress and increase in membership.

First, the minister himself. Never before have we witnessed so many ministers leaving the church and pursuing other fields of activity, such as teaching, or selling insurance, and in some cases, going into full-time counseling work. What is the reason for this exit from the ministry? The reasons again may be legion, sometimes legitimate, but in most cases, totally different reasons. Reasons that are found, not in the congregation, but with the minister himself. The minister is in conflict, not primarily with his education or with his theology. He does not seem to be able to look upon the church as a church built on the Rock, which is Jesus himself. For too many ministers, the church is just another organization for which and in which to work. And if he has been inculcated with the "higher criticism," the minister is prone to preach, not what he believes, but his disbeliefs.

To become acquainted with criticism of the Bible should be the duty of every man going into the ministry. He must, however, keep this criticism from becoming constantly the body of his sermons. The modern congregation is no longer theologically homogeneous, but just the opposite, a mixture of denominations. It takes the congregation only two Sundays to ascertain the leaning of the minister, theologically. In reading the history of pulpiteers of the past, there were many of strong liberal thinking, but when it came to the pulpit, they preached the Word. Why, then, are so many contemporary ministers abdicating? They preach a few years, but soon find they lack what it takes. They have the education, the training in theology, and even one or more degrees, but still cannot hold a church for very long.

What I am now saying may, for many, be a faint echo from long ago. For any young man to go into the ministry without having received a "call" was, in the past, unthinkable. How many times have many of us had to hear the "call" being ridiculed! The new "breed" of ministers rather comes with voice of the Old Testament prophet, "thus speaks the Lord," assuming personal authority in the name of God. It is certainly much easier to preach on social issues than to preach on the Gospel of Jesus Christ. To preach the Word, one has to have an experience with God, an encounter, like thousands have had in the past. One must feel as Paul did, "If we don't speak, these stones must speak." To become a "new creation" through the acceptance of Christ in his life is the first priority of any man who thinks of entering the ministry. Having made this commitment to Christ, he will then be empowered with the Spirit of God to go anywhere to preach "Him Crucified." The Ministry will then become a joy and with every Sunday behind the pulpit, he will share and proclaim the Love of God.

A minister who has made a true commitment to God and the church will never abdicate the ministry. It would be against his very nature to do so. He would not feel at home anywhere else. In fact, to quit the ministry would haunt him forever, because he denied his Savior.

The seminaries will have to come back to the emphasis of "the call" if they are to best serve the church spiritually.

Not all of the churches today have suffered, or are suffering financially, or for lack of attendance. Someone has raised the question, "Why is the membership of the larger denominations decreasing and the membership of the smaller groups increasing?" The answer—the smaller evangelical groups know what they believe and are single-minded in their affirmation.

There are many churches that have a steady and good attendance every Sunday and do not have to resort to many devious means to raise the money to keep going. Why? They preach the Word of God and the need to become a new creation.

To be a Bible-oriented pastor does not mean the exclusion of preaching on social issues or problems of today. The Bible is full of references to injustices and discrimination against one's fellow man. But the Bible emphasizes the change of man from within and not by force or preachments from without. Before society can change, man must change from within. And, we ministers should be the first ones to recognize this fact. It is, of course, much easier to sound off from the pulpit—do this and do that—rather than lead the people in making the change first from within, from a contrite heart. The church simply must return to the preaching of the personal change of heart. First comes the Love of God and then the love of man. When men become born again, they are "new men, born from above," as Jesus said to Nicodemus. They are then men preaching from a turning point, from a solid foundation, that of Christ. This kind of preaching will then be authoritative preaching, preaching from the heart, sincere and to the point. When the minister has been "born of the spirit," the first and most important experience of his life, the second part of his life, the preaching of the Word, will come or follow logically. The two are inseparable; the man of God and the message of God. Where these two are not kept together, neither the minister nor the church have a future.

We celebrate Christmas with enthusiasm, but allow Pentecost to pass unnoticed. If Christmas marks the coming of God in the flesh, Pentecost tells of God the Spirit coming into the lives of the new people of God, the church. Thus, "Christmas is the celebration of God revealing himself in the body of Jesus; Pentecost is the festival of God manifesting himself in a new body—the body of Christ." The preaching and the teaching of Scriptures will never become out-of-date. The verbal proclamation of the faith stands at the center of the lives of the people of God. We may need new forms of communication at times, but these will not replace the proclaiming of God's Word. The proclamation of the Word of God must continue central in the church.

A committed pastor who proclaims the Word of God in his life, from the pulpit and off the pulpit, will never abdicate from the sacred calling of the ministry. He cannot do so; his very nature prevents him from doing so.

CONCLUSION

The anxiety and hesitancy about writing my autobiography is now history too. What I had postponed doing for years is now reality.

To attempt to write the story of one's life is really a rewarding experience. So many events and experiences return to life again, events of great importance that posterity should know about. Our children of today really live in a new world and have no imagination of what life in the early days and in a foreign country was all about.

In the life of this writer, as varied as it was, and in so many countries, a record in some detail was advisable.

May these pages of recorded history of one who sought the promised land in America always be interesting reading. This is my fervent hope and prayer.

LITERATURE

Books

Becker, Rudolph, Serra-Post. Ijuhy, Rio Grande Do Sul, Brazil. *Deutsche Siedler In Rio Grande Do Sul.*
Beratz, Gottlieb. Saratow, 1915. *Die Deutschen Kolonien An Der Unteren Wolga.*
Brendel, Johann. *Aus Den Deutschen Kolonien Im Kutschurganer Gebiet 1930.*
Brepohl, F. W. and W. Fugmann. Stuttgart. *Die Wolhadeutsche Im Brasilianischen Parana, Brazil.*
Brepohl, F. W. Ponta Grossa, Parana, Brazil, 1933. *Geschichten Von Dom Petro II, von Brazilien.*
Gross, F. W. Sacramento, Ca. *Type and Nature of German Publications in North Dakota.*
Hahn, Gottlieb. 35406 Buchdruckerei Joseph Botschner, Hermannstadt. *Die Deutschen Bauernsiedlungen Am Schwarzen Meere.*
Leibbrandt, Gottlieb. Stuttgart, 1928. *Die Auswsnderungen aus Schwaben Nach Russland 1816-1823.*
Leibbrandt, Gottlieb. Stuttgart, 1926. *Die Deutschen Kolonien In Cherson Und Schwaben.*
Schleuning, Johannes, Carol Flemming und C. T. Wiskott. Berlin, 1922. *Aus Tiefer Not—Schicksale Der Deutschen Kolonien in Russland.*
Stempp, Dr. Karl. Stuttgart, 1922. *Die Deutschen Kolonien Im Schwarzmeergebiet.*

Periodicals

"Alto Parana." Jahrbuch von Missiones und Uruguay, 1939.
"Alto Parana." Jahrbuch von Missiones und Paraguay.

"Jahrbuch" 1937 und 1940. Herausgegeben vom Deutschen Volksbund fuer Argentinien, Buenos Aires.

"Der Kirchenbote Kalender 1940." Pioneer Press, Yankton, South Dakota.

"Der Morgenstern," 1930. 4. Jahrgang, Sarata, Russia.

PHOTOGRAPHY, Don Cerveny, Sacramento

About the Author

Fred William Gross was born in Russia in 1895. He emigrated to the United States in 1914, and is a graduate of Redfield College and seminary, Carleton College, and of the University of North Dakota, where he received his master's degree. He was ordained into the Congregational Church in 1922, and married Emilie Bastian in 1924. They have four children—Vernon, Grace, Margie, and Nancy.

Mr. Gross served as a missionary in Argentina and Brazil for six years, and upon returning, was pastor for several churches in California. He was chaplain for the Lodi chapter of the Lions Club and for the American Legion in Lodi, and is a member of the Sacramento County Commission for the Aging. This is his first published book.